THE
4-DIMENSIONAL
MANAGER

THE 4-DIMENSIONAL MANAGER

DiSC Strategies for Managing Different People in the Best Ways

Julie Straw
with Alison Brown Cerier

Produced by Alison Brown Cerier Book Development, Inc.

An Inscape Guide

BERRETT-KOEHLER PUBLISHERS, INC.
San Francisco

Berrett-Koehler Publishers, Inc.
235 Montgomery Street, Suite 650
San Francisco, CA 94104-2916
Tel: (415) 288-0260   Fax: (415) 362-2512   www.bkconnection.com

Ordering Information

Quantity sales. Special discounts are available on quantity purchases by corporations, associations, and others. For details, contact the "Special Sales Department" at the Berrett-Koehler address above.

Individual sales. Berrett-Koehler publications are available through most bookstores. They can also be ordered direct from Berrett-Koehler: Tel: (800) 929-2929; Fax: (802) 864-7626; www.bkconnection.com

Orders for college textbook/course adoption use. Please contact Berrett-Koehler: Tel: (800) 929-2929; Fax: (802) 864-7626.

Orders by U.S. trade bookstores and wholesalers. Please contact Publishers Group West, 1700 Fourth Street, Berkeley, CA 94710. Tel: (510) 528-1444; Fax (510) 528-3444.

Printed in the United States of America
Printed on acid-free and recycled paper that is composed of 80% recovered fiber, including 30% post-consumer waste.

DiSC is a registered trademark of Inscape Publishing, Inc.
Personal Profile System is a registered trademark of Inscape Publishing, Inc.

Library of Congress Cataloging-in-Publication Data
Straw, Julie, 1957-
    The 4-dimensional manager: DiSC strategies for managing different people in the best ways / by Julie Straw with Alison Brown Cerier.
       p. cm.—(An inscape guide)
    ISBN 1-57675-135-X (alk. paper)
    1. Personnel management. 2. Psychology, Industrial.   I Title: Four-dimensional manager. II Cerier, Alison Brown, 1956- III. Title. IV. Series

    HF5549.S8923 2001
    658.3—dc21   2001043700

First Edition
07 06 05 04 03 02   10 9 8 7 6 5 4 3 2 1

Contributing writer: Dorrine Turecamo
Copyeditor: Andrea Chesman
Interior design: Michaelis/Carpelis Design Associates
Cover design: Susan Malikowski, Autographix

Contents

6-18-02

Preface

Do you provide work direction and feedback to others? Do you help others make decisions or solve problems? Are you in a position to motivate or compliment others? If you answered "yes" to any of these questions, you're a manager, whether or not you have the title, and this book is for you.

You are a manager if you are responsible for getting work done through others. You may be at any level of an organization, working formally or informally with employees as well as outside vendors and contractors.

Many managers, especially those who do not have the formal title, have had no training in the skills they need, particularly people skills—yet managing is, above all, about people. When I first became a manager nearly twenty years ago, I was given training on performance reviews, merit increases, and promotions, but not the softer "people skills." I was told what to do, but I had to figure out how to do it.

As a new manager, I decided to follow the Golden Rule: I treated others the way I wanted to be treated. The Golden Rule was a guiding principle in many aspects of my life, and it made sense to follow it when managing others. For example, when I delegated work, I gave the person the amount and kind of direction that I would have liked and needed. When I treated my employees the way I wanted to be treated, some of them responded positively. But to my surprise, some of them didn't respond well. What was going on?

I found the answer in a workshop I took some time later. I was introduced to DiSC, an easy-to-use tool that helps you understand how people think, feel, and act in different situations. DiSC showed me that different people respond to the same situation in different ways. Instead of treating people the way I wanted to be treated, I needed to coach and mentor them as individuals. DiSC helped me build a better relationship with each of my direct reports, and they pulled together as a team. DiSC helped me grow as a manager.

Over and over, I have seen DiSC make a difference. I've had a front-row seat for watching DiSC in action because ten years ago I went to work for Inscape Publishing, the company that publishes the DiSC tool I first used as a new manager. It has been a wonderful opportunity to work with the researchers and product-development team for DiSC and to look for ways to deliver the power of DiSC to people and organizations around the world.

As a manager, you play a key role in your organization's success by motivating other people, guiding and directing their work activities, and recognizing and rewarding their accomplishments. To be effective, you have to take the time to get to know each one of them.

You may be wondering how you will possibly find time to work with individual differences. DiSC will make the learning easy, quick, and practical. By focusing on the four dimensions of DiSC, you'll be able to better understand each person you are managing. With DiSC as your "golden rule," you'll be able to treat each person individually and be more successful.

You will start with you. The first part of this book will help you discover your usual managerial style. Then you'll focus on the people you're working with. From there, you can decide if adapting your behavior might help you get the best results for yourself, for the person you are managing, and for your organization. There will be chapters on applying DiSC to basic managerial tasks.

Today, I continue to use the four DiSC dimensions when managing others and in my relationships with co-workers, family, and friends. I've also taught thousands of trainers and consultants about Inscape's DiSC model at conferences and training seminars around the world. Every time I present DiSC, I have the pleasure of watching people realize that different isn't good or bad; different is just different. DiSC gives people an easy way to understand why they respond a certain way and why other people might respond differently.

Whether you are a new manager or have been at it for a while, I know that understanding DiSC and getting to know others will bring new dimensions to the way you manage.

Julie Straw
Inscape Publishing

Acknowledgments

This book could not have happened without a team effort. I would like to thank Pat Benson for her vision, persistence, and patience in making this book, and the others in the Inscape Guide Series, a reality. My thanks to Tom Ritchey, Pamela Cole, and Miriam Kragness for sharing their DiSC expertise with me. I am grateful for the talent of Alison Brown Cerier, for her ability to weave my stories together to create a coherent, organized book. I am also grateful to Steven Piersanti and the team at Berrett-Koehler for their partnership and commitment to quality.

Over the years, countless people have showed me that using DiSC in managing not only makes good business sense, but builds great friendships along the way. Among these people are Deb Peters Splett, Diane Larson, Stuart Rosen, Frank Mazzacco, Kay LaFleur, and the entire team at Inscape Publishing.

I want to thank Jim Straw for his belief in me through all the ups and downs. And lastly, I dedicate this book to my son Andy, who did learn how to tell time, even after all those "Just one more minute, Andy" excuses turned into hours.

Why 1-Dimensional Managing Isn't Enough

Eli manages the central reservations center of a worldwide hotel chain. During a recent promotion, the call center was swamped with twice as many incoming calls as usual. Everybody was working overtime and taking fewer breaks. Unlike peak times in the past, morale stayed high.

Eli looked for reasons why and realized that two people had stepped forward to make a difference. One was Lauren. Two weeks into the busy time, when the stress was starting to get to everybody, Lauren had offered to bring in lunch—then surprised everyone by putting the lunches in a conference room decorated with balloons and pulsing with great tunes. Everybody enjoyed their short break—Lauren most of all. The next Friday, she did it again, this time putting the lunches on blankets spread out under the trees behind the parking lot.

Eli saw that Juanita had made a very different but equally important contribution. She had volunteered to construct a special schedule to make sure everybody had a fair share of breaks and late hours.

When the promotion was over, Eli brought everybody together to celebrate the group's efforts and to acknowledge Lauren's and Juanita's special work. He announced, "Lauren and Juanita both did a fabulous job. Without them, we would never have been able to handle the calls this last month. Let's have a round of applause for Lauren and Juanita!"

Lauren pumped both fists in the air and let out a whoop. She was loving the attention. Juanita smiled and said, "Thank you," but when Eli looked for her a few minutes later, he found that she'd left the room.

Next month, the workload returned to normal. When Eli went over the phone reports, he found that Lauren's call level was at an all-time high, but Juanita's had dropped dramatically. Now that he thought about it, ever since the special celebration, Lauren had seemed more enthusiastic than ever, but Juanita had been rather withdrawn.

Eli had complimented two people the same way, but they had responded in two different ways. He had been successful exactly half of the time.

He had been a 1-dimensional manager: He had used the same managing approach with everyone.

Most people tend to manage others the way they themselves prefer to be managed. For example, Eli had given the kind of compliment *he* loved best: public, effusive, enthusiastic. He had been thrilled when he was named manager of the year at the company's recognition day. He used this style all the time; he liked to walk through the call center tossing out comments, like "You're doing great."

Eli's style hit home with some people—Lauren, for example. Lauren loved to be the center of attention. Bring on the applause!

Juanita was looking for something different. Juanita wanted to be recognized for the competence, logic, and hard work she'd invested in the complex schedule. Instead of a generalized, public display, she was looking for specific recognition. She would have cherished a detailed memo. While Eli's praise was sincere, she considered it empty flattery, thinking he didn't quite realize just what she had done for the group.

The trouble with 1-dimensional managing is that it doesn't work all the time.

Doing What Comes Naturally

Like Eli, most managers tend to approach similar situations in similar ways. They stick with a certain way of delegating, problem-solving, coaching, giving feedback, communicating, and more. We're talking not about *what* they do, but *how* they do it.

You, too, have a usual approach that seems natural and comfortable. When you use this approach, you're managing from your strengths. Consider Eli. He enjoyed giving kudos, and he was good at it. At the congratulatory gathering, he was more than comfortable—he was loving it. He would have been far less comfortable sitting down to write a detailed, precise memo for Juanita.

Your natural style has many sources, including your genes, background, education, and work experience. Over the years, it has been shaped by ongoing feedback. You stick with what's worked before.

Your natural style is your "first dimension."

In this book, you will be introduced to a practical tool that will help you discover your natural style, or first dimension. This tool, called DiSC, allows you to focus on and understand how you are thinking, feeling, and acting in a variety of work situations, including managing. In the next chapter, you'll use DiSC to focus on a management situation that is troubling you right now. DiSC will give you a chance to step back from the situation and learn about yourself.

There are four basic styles of thinking, feeling, and acting. Through DiSC, you will discover which of these styles you are using.

Who will teach you about yourself? You. Who knows you better? *You are the expert on you.*

DiSC is no gimmick. It has been researched and refined for nearly thirty years. DiSC has been used across North America and translated and validated for many other countries. Thousands of companies and organizations, big and small, have used DiSC. In fact, trainers and consultants have used DiSC in workshops attended by more than 40 million people. DiSC takes only a few minutes, and you can put the results to work right away.

They Are Not You

When you take DiSC, you will focus on your own response to a situation. Later in the book, you'll look at how the people you manage are responding to the same situation. You can't go inside other people's heads to know what they are thinking and feeling. Once you are familiar with DiSC, however, you will recognize many clues in the way people are behaving in a situation. These behaviors reflect thoughts and feelings and will allow you to see helpful patterns.

You'll see right away that people respond to common workplace situations in a range of ways. For example, some people feel comfortable with change, while others loathe it. Some love competition and others run from it. People react differently to rules, fact checking, socializing, feedback, deadlines, teamwork, and other situations. And that's why they respond to your natural style of managing in different ways.

Ann is the manager of a small computer-components company. She describes four people she is currently managing. Perhaps some of this will seem familiar to you.

"Andy works in order processing. He goes over each item again and again to make sure it's right. His carefulness is great, but work is stacking up behind him. A new customer just sent back a shipment—it was the third time we'd delivered late.

"Kathy is our marketing director. She loves to launch new campaigns, but the initiatives fizzle out. She gets antsy when it's detail time.

"Every time I walk past Marie's door, someone's pouring out his or her troubles. Her office is practically a counseling center. I'm supposed to hand in budget projections for the third quarter, and I've been waiting for Marie's numbers for a week now.

"Since Burt started running the production line, he's been making lots of big changes. Some of his innovations are great, but quality is down because he doesn't take the time to think things through."

Differences, difficult as they may be at times, are the makings of an exceptional company. When every detail counts, you need conscientious people like Andy. An inspiring person like Kathy has invaluable people skills and can get the team pumped up every time. People feel comfortable bringing their concerns to a sensitive, tactful person like Marie. She knows what's really going on, and she can help people think things through and feel better. Burt is a powerful force for change, and he drives the group toward the goal. As a manager, Ann has the job of managing those differences.

Oh, those differences. While Ann would readily acknowledge the contributions of each of the four people she described, she would also be quick to admit that each of them drives her crazy sometimes. She has found each one difficult to work with at times, no matter how hard she has tried. There have been frustrations, stress, sometimes anger. There have been misunderstandings, compromised results, out-and-out conflict, or just vaguely muffled, unsatisfactory outcomes.

You, too, may be struggling with situations involving a perfectionist Andy, a wildly enthusiastic Kathy, a counseling Marie, or a take-charge Burt. How will you make it all hum?

Looking at the Situation

DiSC begins with self-awareness, but it doesn't end there. It also develops "other-awareness" and "situation-awareness." DiSC is about self, other, and situation: SOS. It's not about me and it's not about you; it's about us together.

When you tune in to someone else's style of behavior in a situation, you may discover that the person isn't behaving at all the way *you* would. Often this is the source of those misunderstandings, missteps, and missed goals. What does this individual need? What are his or her strengths? What motivates this person? How can you help this person do his or her best work so you get the results the organization expects?

When you look at a particular situation and everyone involved through the lens of DiSC, you may believe that your natural style is the best managing style. You'll see which strengths will be assets in this situation.

On the other hand, you may come to believe that your natural, first-dimensional style may not work this time. DiSC will suggest ways you might choose a different style to get the best outcome for yourself, for the person you are managing, and for your organization. This is called adapting.

Adapting does not mean that you are wishy-washy; it means that you choose the most appropriate, effective ways to address the situation. It does not mean you bend over backwards for your staff; it does mean that you understand and respect another person's special talents, concerns, limitations, and roadblocks. This allows you to work together to get the job done.

Adapting doesn't mean changing who you or others are. It means responding to the needs of a particular situation—when you choose to.

For example, let's say you are delegating a project. Your usual way is to bottom-line it. You tell the person the results needed and the time line, then leave him or her alone to get the job done. As you reflect on the person you want to hand something over to today, you become convinced that that approach wouldn't work at all. This person needs and wants detailed, step-by-step directions. DiSC knowledge can help you determine the amount and type of information to communicate when delegating, and the best way to follow up.

Choosing the managing style that's best for a particular situation is called 4-dimensional managing. This is a skill that every manager can learn. You can use DiSC to help someone you manage make a decision, solve a problem, or feel more motivated. DiSC can also help you reward high performance or give constructive criticism. This is a tool that you can put to work every day as you do the tough and rewarding work of managing.

While you are considering ways you might act on what you learn, think small. Usually the best way to move forward is to take baby steps. Often if you take a small step toward meeting the needs of someone you manage, he or she will take a big step toward you. If you move a little, often you won't have to move farther. But before you can take a step, you need to know in which direction to go. You need to take in some data, and that's where DiSC comes in.

What 4-Dimensional Managing Can Do for You

Wonderful things will happen when you move from 1-dimensional managing to 4-dimensional managing.

First, you will have a tool for understanding "people problems." While most managers tend to focus on what needs to be done and when, the greatest challenges are not the schedule or the resources or the goals, but all those messy, complex interactions among the people doing the work. DiSC will help you understand the human issues.

Then, after you've clarified the various points of view, you'll discover your options for managing this situation. It's natural to fall into your usual way of approaching a person or task—but that's not always effective. Using

DiSC can take you off automatic pilot. Instead of always relying on your 1-dimension style, you take a few moments to consider what's best in this situation. That process of stepping back and reflecting can make all the difference for you.

Managing in the other three dimensions may feel uncomfortable at first, but the more you do it, the more confident you will feel when you stretch and adapt.

Everyone knows the parable of the reed and the mighty oak. The oak tree thought it was stronger than the reed, since it had stood tall and straight through many winters, while the reed bent with every breeze. Then came a violent storm. Afterward, the oak was toppled, but the reed sprang back. The moral is that there is strength in flexibility. Instead of being a mighty but vulnerable oak tree, you can be a reed that may bend in different directions but will always spring back up. As a 4-dimensional manager, you will have flexibility and resilience, and this will increase the chances that you will weather every storm.

Here's another visual image. Picture a 1-dimensional manager as a flat cardboard cutout stuck into a slot. Not much is holding up the manager. Someone can come along and easily push it over. The manager is vulnerable. Now put the manager into a stand that's braced by long boards in four directions. That manager would be tough to push over. In the many work situations that can flatten a manager, your four dimensions will be your support system.

A 4-dimensional manager has the insight and range to be effective in the workplace, where people are indeed different.

Discovering Your Style

It's time to use DiSC to reflect on a real situation you're facing. You will respond to a list of short phrases that describe the various ways you are feeling, thinking, and acting in this situation.

Does this sound too much like a test? Don't worry—this is *not* a test. There are no right or wrong answers. You can't pass or fail DiSC, and it doesn't predict success or failure. DiSC is not about testing and fixing, but discovering and capitalizing. DiSC is a way for you to understand yourself a little better. You will tell yourself about you. DiSC will help you interpret and apply what you see.

It's not a test. So relax and enjoy this time.

In This Situation

For meaningful and useful results, choose a specific management situation as your focus. Don't focus on a one-time incident or a particular five-minute interaction. Nor should you pick an overly general situation, like "managing." Also, it isn't useful to treat the tool as an oracle and ask it a question about the future ("Will Alice ever work up to her potential?"). It is best to think about an ongoing problem or situation. An appropriate focus would be "managing Beth on project X" or "delegating to Steve."

Consider your focus situation. How did you feel, think, and behave? Who else was involved? Was the location or time important? Recall what happened, what was said and done. Then focus on what *you* were thinking and feeling and how you were acting as the situation was happening.

It's worthwhile to spend time choosing and developing your focus. The more details you can recall about your experience, the better. Sum up the highlights in a brief sentence that will be easy to remember. It's too hard to hold a whole paragraph in your mind while using the tool.

Instructions

Pages 12 and 13 present a list of phrases. For each phrase, select the number from 5 to 1 that best indicates how accurately or inaccurately it describes your feelings, thoughts, and behaviors in your focus situation. Write the number in the box to the right of the phrase.

It is critical that you use the full range of numbers: 5, 4, 3, 2, and 1. The value—*to you*—of your responses will depend on how precisely you weight each response. It will pay to reflect before rating each phrase. Don't worry—the tool is brief. It takes most people about ten minutes to finish.

If you think a particular phrase isn't relevant to your focus situation, spend an extra minute considering it before putting down a 1. The tool is designed so that the phrases are related in some way to almost every situation.

Be sure to respond to every phrase.

Your Personal DiSC Instrument

- *Focus on a situation*
- *Reflect on your responses*
- *Discover your managerial style*

Inscape Publishing

Working across the four columns on both pages, write after each phrase the number that best describes you in this situation. 1 = Very inaccurate or does not apply 2 = Inaccurate 3 = Neither accurate nor inaccurate 4 = Accurate 5 = Very accurate

good listener		want to make the rules	
put up with things I don't like		go straight ahead with projects	
willing to follow orders		act in a forceful way	
will go along with others		want to win	
think of others before I decide		will be the first to act	
willing to help		do not give in	
understand others' feelings		people see me as powerful	
nice to other people		sure of myself	
have warm feelings for people		want to be in charge	
let others lead		like to take action	
don't like to cause problems		quick to act	
don't make demands of people		feel strong	
Total column 1		**Total column 2**	
Subtract	-1	Add	+2
Score	●	Score	▪

like to do things accurately		wide variety of friends	
like doing things the right way		liked by others	
do things right the first time		like to meet people	
think of what makes sense		fun to be with	
like to be precise		see things positively	
shy with others		feel contented	
good at analyzing things		happy and carefree	
think things through		liven things up	
keep things to myself		feel relaxed most of the time	
think things over carefully		happy most of the time	
don't like too much attention		find it easy to meet strangers	
don't say much in a group		communicate in a lively manner	
Total column 3		**Total column 4**	
	+0	Subtract	-2
Score	☽	Score	◆

Scoring

Add up the scores in each column, if you haven't done so already. Adjust the scores by adding or subtracting as shown, and you'll have four totals matched with symbols. Each symbol corresponds to one of the four DiSC dimensions of behavior:

- ● stands for Supportiveness
- ▥ stands for Dominance
- ☾ stands for Conscientiousness
- ◆ stands for Influence

The columns are in the order S, D, C, and I. Since we'll be talking about DiSC, not SDCI, let's unscramble your score now. Write your adjusted score for each dimension on the blank lines in the Tally Box.

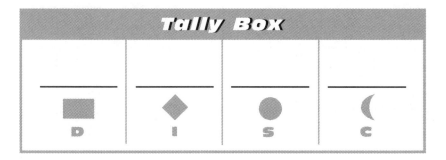

The DiSC Dimensions

Your feelings, thoughts, and behavior in your focus situation reflect varying levels of the four DiSC dimensions:

- **D**ominance
- **I**nfluence
- **S**upportiveness
- **C**onscientiousness

One dimension—your highest score—is playing the greatest role. Go to the Tally Box and circle your high score. (If there are two equally high scores, circle both.)

Below are descriptions of the four dimensions. Start by reading the description for your highest score. Then read about the other three dimensions.

Dominance (D)

The Dominance dimension shows itself in direct, decisive behavior.

Goal achievement. If in this situation your highest dimension is D, you think it's important to meet goals. In this situation, you don't like to be told what to do. You set high standards, make your own rules, and feel like a champ when you meet your goals.

Acting decisively. You feel confident you can get things done quickly. You grow impatient when a project takes too long to get going. If things aren't going as smoothly as you would like, you may take charge. You don't ignore risks, but you aren't afraid to take a calculated gamble, since you know risks can pay off.

Winning. You enjoy competition. You play to win.

Directness. You can be blunt sometimes. You take pride in coming to the point and speaking directly. In this situation, you are not likely to have patience with incompetent people or those who seem unwilling to change.

Influence (I)

The Influence dimension shows itself in optimistic, outgoing behavior.

Communication. In this situation, you're a "people person." You are the consummate networker. You relish opportunities to share your enthusiasm and ideas. You like to meet new people and pull them together. People enjoy having you around because you communicate easily and in a lively way. You make the party.

Participation. You participate actively in a group. Even though you probably like being in the limelight, you don't necessarily want to take the lead. You have warm feelings for others.

Thinking positively. You feel optimistic about the situation. You see the best in people and situations.

Supportiveness (S)

The Supportiveness dimension shows itself in sympathetic, cooperative behavior.

Helping others. In this situation, you want to make things easier or better for others. You're a good listener, and others tend to confide in you. You respect this confidence and give them your time. You feel genuine warmth and empathy for others.

Fitting in. You don't like conflict. You'll avoid arguments whenever you can.

Working behind the scenes. You prefer not to stand out in a group. You enjoy making a difficult task easier or quietly helping to relieve stress or pain. Helping others meet their goals may be an important way for you to meet your own goals.

Preservation. In this situation, you want to think things over before making a change. You would rather respect the past and preserve what has already been accomplished than replace the tried-and-true with the untested.

Conscientiousness (C)

The Conscientiousness dimension shows itself in concerned, correct behavior.

Doing things right. In this situation, you want to make sure no mistakes are made. You value your reputation for being reliable and trustworthy.

Planning ahead. Once you know the goal, you spend time planning the best way to meet it. You'll consider all facts and figures. You often point out problems before they even happen.

Thinking clearly. You pay attention and see things others might miss.

Privacy. You often prefer to work alone or with a few others you can trust.

Multidimensional You

Did one of the descriptions sound just like the way you are responding to this situation? That is more likely if one dimension was much higher than the others. There will be times, though, when two or even three dimensions are playing a strong role, so you may not see a true fit until you identify your more complete DiSC response pattern in the next chapter.

Each of us has within us some level of *all* the styles. We're multidimensional. You can draw on any of your dimensions to understand other people. You also can choose to draw on a dimension to adapt your behavior to meet the needs of a situation. As a manager, you can decide to call on your other dimensions as you work with individuals on your staff who have styles different from your own.

The lower dimensions may emerge more strongly when you take DiSC again with a different focus. DiSC identifies a style of thoughts, feelings, and behavior *in a specific situation*. Think about how you would feel and act if you were meeting a potential client for the first time. Different than if you were having lunch with a buddy you've worked with for years? What if your team had fallen short of its goals, and your boss was calling you in to talk about it?

Here's an example of one manager responding to two different situations in two different ways. Nick, a senior partner in a small law firm, managed six attorneys who handled litigation. When a case was in the research phase, Nick responded with high-C. He pushed his team to uncover every bit of evidence and precedence. At the team meeting right before the court date, though, he responded as an I. He'd always enjoyed arguing cases and was known as a fiery litigator. At the meeting, he pumped up the team members so they were confident in their abilities to win the case. Though he no longer presented cases personally, Nick still grew animated when a court date approached, and he passed along his energy to the people he managed.

Because different situations can bring out different styles of behavior, DiSC is designed to be taken again and again as new situations arise. Think about a second situation at work, then take DiSC again. Score your results and compare them to the first results.

Some people wonder what low dimensions say about them. If you scored low on a dimension, the situation might not call for that dimension, so the specific phrases didn't seem relevant. If a dimension isn't high in your response pattern, that doesn't mean that you are showing the opposite of that dimension. For example, someone who is not high in D isn't necessarily indirect or indecisive. That person is just not describing himself or herself as more direct or decisive in this situation.

Not a Personality Type

Over time, you may find that one or more of your dimensions are often high. While it can be useful to spot patterns in your responses, don't assume that DiSC has identified something set and permanent about you—a core personality. What you have just taken is not a personality test. DiSC does not tell you your personality type.

Personality begins with a unique genetic makeup and forms as a person has life experiences. Personality is our hardwiring. It has many facets; for example, some people are extroverted, and some are introverted, and they always will be. We don't get to choose our personalities. They come out of how we were brought up, what we were taught in school, our experiences, and the mental and emotional equipment our genes set up for us.

There are a number of tools for measuring personality. Most widely known is the Myers-Briggs Type Indicator.

DiSC does not reveal your core personality type. Instead, it reveals how your personality is responding to your environment. Personality is, at most, half of the equation. The other half is the environment. Personality and the environment (or situation) interact and produce thoughts, feelings, and behaviors.

DiSC is not psychotherapy, and it won't reveal the mysteries of your inner being. But many situations call for immediate action, not long-term analysis. DiSC can help you take appropriate action to meet the needs of the situation and everyone involved.

While you can't change your personality, you can choose to change the way you respond to situations. That difference makes DiSC a practical tool.

Keeping the situational nature of DiSC in mind will help you avoid the labeling trap. Labeling is the affixing of a permanent DiSC designation on yourself or others. Instead of saying, "She is responding in a D way" or "My D is up," a person who labels others says, "She's a D" or "I'm D." Labeling leads to assumptions like these:

- I'm a D. I make the decisions. Why should anyone expect that I'd be interested in talking things over?
- Let's not invite Rachel to the meeting. She's so C she'll nit-pick the project to death.

Labeling puts limits on yourself and others. It can become a convenient excuse for not trying to work things out. It's fairer and more effective to think of yourself and others as multidimensional and capable of responding to different situations in different ways.

The Two Questions

The four DiSC responses reflect the different ways that people subconsciously answer two questions about a situation:

- Is this situation favorable or unfavorable to me?
- Do I have power or control in this situation?

Your feelings about the environment and your power in it are the underpinnings of the style of behavior you show in any situation.

When you took DiSC the first time, did the focus situation feel challenging or comfortable? In other words, did you sense the environment as *favorable* or *unfavorable* for you?

Let's say you were feeling respected and trusted. You had worked with the person for some time, and the work was generally going well. Chances are you felt at ease. Your manner was relaxed. You were comfortable and unconcerned. You thought you were in a *favorable* environment.

If the situation was giving feedback to someone who had made a major mistake, you probably felt that the environment was not favorable. In an *unfavorable* environment, you will feel on guard, ill at ease, or uncomfortable. You may feel you're being sized up or challenged. A situation can also feel unfavorable because it's new for you.

Next, did you feel that you had the ability to control or change the situation, or not? Whether or not the situation was favorable, could you make it better?

Your assessments of the environment and your perceived power were behind the style of behavior you used in that situation. Each combination of yes and no answers is unique to a DiSC style.

- People who believe that the environment is not favorable, but that they can control or change it, are likely to use the Dominance style of behavior.
- People who feel that the environment is favorable, and that they can control or change it, are likely to use the Influence style.
- People who feel that the environment is favorable, but that they lack power, are likely to use the Supportiveness style.
- People who feel that the environment is not favorable, and that they lack power, are likely to use the Conscientiousness style.

The Research behind DiSC

Why should you trust what the DiSC tool is telling you?

Here's some background on the research behind this tool. DiSC began with a theory of human behavior that was first advanced in the 1920s by American psychologist William Moulton Marston. Marston was interested not in mental illness, but in how normal people felt and behaved as they interacted with the world around them. Based on his pioneering research, Marston developed a model of normal behavior that identified four distinct dimensions of behavior. In 1972, Inscape Publishing, a Minneapolis-based research and publishing firm, used Marston's work as the foundation for further research that resulted in the *Personal Profile System,* a learning instrument that gave people unprecedented access to an understanding of their own feelings and behavior in almost any situation.

DiSC at a Glance

D (Dominance)
- Getting immediate results
- Taking action
- Accepting challenges
- Making decisions quickly
- Questioning the status quo
- Solving problems

I (Influence)
- Contacting people
- Verbalizing
- Generating enthusiasm
- Entertaining people
- Viewing people and situations optimistically
- Participating in a group

S (Supportiveness)
- Performing in a consistent, predictable way
- Showing patience
- Wanting to help others
- Showing loyalty
- Being a good listener
- Creating a stable, harmonious work environment

C (Conscientiousness)
- Paying attention to key directives and standards
- Concentrating on key details
- Weighing pros and cons
- Checking for accuracy
- Analyzing performance critically
- Using a systematic approach

Inscape Publishing continued to refine and improve the *Personal Profile System* through ongoing research throughout the 1990s, using thousands of demographically and professionally diverse respondents. This book and the other books in this series are the first time that Inscape's DiSC tools are available outside the professional training and development environment.

A learning tool like DiSC can provide useful feedback only if *it measures what it claims to measure (validity) and if it does so consistently (reliability)*. Many tools, though often used by good companies, lack even minimal validity and reliability. In contrast, Inscape Publishing uses research to ensure that our tools provide you with accurate and meaningful information.

When researchers assess the quality of an instrument, they first consider the sample population. If the sample were white male accountants from Kansas, then the instrument would only be appropriate for use by white male accountants from Kansas. Inscape Publishing ensures that our research samples are representative of people of different ages and racial backgrounds and from a wide variety of occupations and geographical locations.

Tools also have to be reliable, which means that the results must be consistent. Professional-quality instruments offer "scale reliability" greater than .70. The numbers for Inscape's DiSC range from .77 to .85.

A high-quality behavioral tool also offers validity; in other words, *it measures what it is said to measure*. Validity was emphasized in creating both the scales and the response-pattern feedback. The validity of Inscape's DiSC scales has been confirmed by two types of statistical analyses, factor analysis and multidimensional scaling.

For more details, see "The Research behind DiSC" at the back of the book.

How You Manage Yourself and Others

The last chapter described the four DiSC dimensions of behavior: Dominance, Influence, Supportiveness, and Conscientiousness. Does one of these closely mirror the way you responded to the situation? Or was something else at work here?

That "something else" is another one, perhaps two, dimensions that were also playing a strong role. While your results probably showed at least some level of each of the four dimensions, numbers at a certain level make a difference.

These high dimensions define your DiSC response pattern in this situation. Your DiSC response pattern will more fully describe how you are feeling, thinking, and acting in the situation. It will allow you to explore how you are managing yourself and others.

Your DiSC Response Pattern

Look back at your Tally Box in chapter 2. Any total equal to or higher than 44 is a high score. In the first column below, write your highest score. Below it, put the first letter of that dimension (D, I, S, or C). If you have a second high score, write it in the second column; and so on. The cutoff number is absolute. Don't fudge by circling a dimension that's just shy of the cutoff.

Your DiSC Response Pattern				
Score 44 or above, starting with highest				
Dimension				

Five kinds of results are possible:

1. A single pattern consisting of one high dimension.
2. A double combination, in which two styles meet or exceed the cutoff.
3. A triple combination, in which three styles meet or exceed the cutoff.
4. No number meets or exceeds the cutoff.
5. All four numbers meet or exceed the cutoff.

DiSC combination patterns, the doubles and triples, combine aspects of two or three styles in fascinating ways. The combinations are not the result of simple addition, like piling one building block on top of another. They're more like baking a cake; you mix varying amounts of separate ingredients, put them in the oven, and end up with something new.

For most of the combinations, the order of the dimensions doesn't matter; for example, IC is the same pattern as CI. Order does make a difference in two cases. DI and ID are two different patterns, as are SI and IS.

If all four of your scores meet or exceed the cutoff number. The situation you have chosen as your focus may be one in which you feel that you need to be all things to all people. It is also possible that you believed that you were *supposed to* respond in a certain way, whether you really felt that way or not, so you rated almost all of the phrases as Accurate or Very Accurate. Remember, there are no right or wrong answers. Take the instrument again (there is an additional copy at the back of the book), either focusing more closely on this situation or choosing a new one. Slow down. Think carefully about each phrase. Use the full range of responses.

If none of your scores meets or exceeds the cutoff number. It is likely that the situation you have chosen is difficult for you to keep in focus. It is also possible that you skipped some phrases or may think that some of the phrases do not apply to the situation you have chosen. Check over the instrument to make certain that you haven't skipped anything, and remember that the instrument is designed so that almost all of the phrases apply *in some way* to any situation. Retake the instrument, this time focusing more closely on the chosen situation or choosing a new one. There is no time limit, so give yourself enough time to think carefully about each phrase. Try to use the full range of responses.

How Common?

Among the research sample population, the following percentages represent the number of people who had each response pattern. The numbers don't add up to 100 because some people had no scores above the cutoff number of 44, or all scores above the cutoffs. As you can see, most people had a double or triple response pattern.

D	6%	SI	3%
I	2%	IS	4%
S	3%	IC	1%
C	7%	SC	12%
DI	3%	DIS	7%
ID	6%	IDC	5%
DS	1%	DSC	5%
DC	8%	ISC	12%

Getting to Know You

Whether your pattern is single, double, or triple, read the rest of this chapter, which explores the single patterns. This will deepen your understanding of the four dimensions. Why learn about them all? First, you will encounter people who use each of these styles. Second, since DiSC is situational, when you take the instrument with a different focus, you may have different results. And third, you may need to draw on one of your other dimensions to resolve a situation.

The combination patterns are described toward the end of the book. While it's important to read the sections on the single patterns, you don't have to—and probably shouldn't—read all of the sections about the combinations. If you have a double or triple pattern, it will be more useful and less confusing to go next to the section that discusses your combination and focus on it exclusively.

For both the single and combination patterns, the profile begins with a general description of how you are probably feeling, acting, or behaving in that situation. Then there are observations about ways your style can bring value to the situation, insights you may want to share with others, and things to watch out for.

Each profile includes lists of phrases describing various ways that your pattern may be expressing itself. The lists focus on *various ways your style may affect how you manage yourself and others.* They are:

- **Motivates You.** People are motivated by different things. Some crave recognition, some a challenge, some a chance to help others. Each DiSC response pattern is associated with particular motivating factors. How many of the motivating factors for your pattern are in your current work environment? If there aren't as many as you would like, you may want to take steps to meet more of your needs.
- **Demotivates You.** How can you eliminate some of these factors from your work environment? How are they affecting the way you see the situation?
- **Your Preferred Environment.** What one person finds delightful, another finds intolerable. People using this response pattern tend to like an environment with certain characteristics. You can use this list of characteristics to reflect on actions you might take to make your work environment more closely match your personal preferences. As you do, think about whether the environment of your focus situation is one in which you feel comfortable.
- **You Avoid or Dislike.** People tend to avoid things that make them feel uncomfortable. What have you been avoiding about

this situation? You may be able to spare yourself some tasks you don't like. On the other hand, you may want to consider whether you might become a more effective manager if you stopped avoiding them so often.

- **To Be More Effective.** Your response style may be viewed as a strength or a weakness, depending on the situation. This section suggests actions you might take to become a more effective manager. Suggestions may include taking another approach or thinking about the situation in a different way. As with all of DiSC, you will decide what is right for you and your situation.

D: Direct and Decisive

In this situation, you are tackling the task head-on, confident others will follow. Power is primary to you. If your authority is challenged, you will take action to get what you want. You must be in control. You can identify with race car drivers who report that they're most unnerved not when speeding around the track at two hundred miles per hour, but when making a pit stop—because they're no longer in control, the work crew is. You may be quick to be demanding or critical. "Spare me the details," you say. "Just give me the results I want." *In this situation:*

You love a challenge. If you're guaranteed full control, you're the first to volunteer. You can't wait to get to work and get things done. You'll *make* it go. When you say, "The buck stops here," you mean it. You're not afraid to ask the tough questions, and you'll persist until they're answered. Even when someone else is designated chair of a committee or team, you generally end up in charge because you're the one who moves things along.

You're on the move. You want to have the fastest computer, the latest software. You love your cell phone, e-mail, and other technologies that help you get the job done.

It bugs you when other people take a long time to make up their minds. They dawdle over details and paperwork, or idly chitchat. You want to interrupt and say, "Stick to the point. Let's not get off track."

Dominance Style

Motivates You
- Control over your work environment
- Directing other people's activities
- New opportunities and challenges
- Opportunities for advancement

Demotivates You
- Being questioned or overruled
- Limited responsibility for results
- Restricted access to resources
- Close supervision

Your Preferred Environment
- Maximum freedom to determine how things are done
- Fast-paced
- Results-oriented

You Avoid or Dislike
- Appearing soft or weak
- Routine, predictable situations
- Being micromanaged

To Be More Effective
- Instead of just announcing your conclusions, explain how you got there.
- Recognize the efforts of others.
- Take more time to think through consequences before going ahead.

Are you taking enough time to think things through before launching full speed ahead? Are you taking enough time to explain to others how you reached your conclusions? Attending to people's feelings can encourage them to feel more enthusiastic about your plan. Thinking things through can prevent a major disaster. Both steps, which you tend to blow past, could be a good investment of your time.

You want full control over your resources. Close supervision is hard for you to take. If you have to report frequently on your activities, you feel you are being treated like a child. If you can't have freedom, you feel tied up. If you're in a situation where you're required to do routine work with little or no variety, you're probably unhappy. And if you think there's no opportunity for advancement, you may not be interested in your work at all.

You approach conflicts head-on. If you can, you may pull rank to end a conflict. If you have to fire someone, your strategy is to "be direct, state the facts briefly, then walk out." Sure, it's easier for you, but is it easier for the other person?

Unfortunately, your directness will overpower some people. You might want to work on your skills of tact, diplomacy, and negotiation—especially on win-win strategies.

I: Optimistic and Outgoing

You are focused on the people involved in this situation. You enjoy talking and working with them. You are an inspiring, enthusiastic, optimistic force. *In this situation:*

You believe in meetings. They can be brief and impromptu or planned well in advance. You see meetings as a useful tool. You love calling meetings on the spur of the moment so people's reactions will be fresh and spontaneous. You value get-togethers because everyone has a chance to speak out and give their opinions.

You think work should be fun. You wonder if some people ever let go and laugh. You don't like to work with people who are unfriendly or who give one-word answers to your questions.

Influence Style

Motivates You
- Dialoguing with others
- Immediate verbal feedback
- Enthusiastic recognition
- Acknowledgment of your feelings

Demotivates You
- Reserved or unfriendly co-workers
- Rigid schedules
- Pessimism
- Routine, detailed tasks

Your Preferred Environment
- Fast-paced
- Positive feedback and recognition
- Lots of variety and creativity

You Avoid or Dislike
- Conflict
- Losing approval
- Detailed or repetitive tasks
- Working alone

To Be More Effective
- Develop time-management skills.
- Be realistic when evaluating people and situations.
- Rein in impulsive responses that can escalate the situation.

Details and repetitive tasks make you antsy. While you're great at generating creative ideas, you're probably weak on the follow-through. Instead of doing all your homework, you may try to steamroll your plans through with the force of your personality. But details do matter. Back up your brilliant ideas with facts and examples. You will be a more effective manager if you work on developing organized, systematic methods for putting your ideas into action. Then follow through on key details more consistently. It's not always enough to say, "Trust me!"

You enjoy networking and schmoozing. You spend a lot of time in meetings, on the phone, and enjoying conversations with your work buddies. Business-oriented socializing can build valuable work relationships, but are you making the most of your valuable time?

You'd cross the street to avoid a fight. Confrontations make you uncomfortable. You want everyone to be friends, but it's not realistic to expect that everyone will always get along. Try to see conflict as a chance to address important issues. With your excellent people skills, you're up to the challenge!

S: Sympathetic and Cooperative

In this situation, you are probably going out of your way to be helpful to others. Cooperation is your middle name. You're fair and reasonable. If there's a misunderstanding, you're confident things can be worked out. You like an orderly environment with clearly defined responsibility and authority. *In this situation:*

If something works, you stick with it. You don't believe in change for the sake of change. Over time you can adjust to something new, but if a procedure has been serving you well, you prefer to keep it. Taking the time to learn a new computer program makes no sense to you unless it can measurably improve the way you do your job. You don't rush into things. Although change has never come easily to you, if the reasons for it are sound and fully explained, you'll support the change to avoid causing conflict.

Supportive Style

Motivates You
- Cooperating with others
- Clearly defined responsibility and authority
- Providing good service
- Job security

Demotivates You
- Rapid, unpredictable change
- Competitiveness and aggressiveness
- Lack of support from managers or co-workers
- Confrontation

Your Preferred Environment
- Predictable and orderly
- Harmonious, informal, and friendly

You Avoid or Dislike
- Unpredictable or uncertain situations
- Disorganized and disorderly workplaces

To Be More Effective
- Take small steps toward becoming more flexible about routines and changes.
- Learn some techniques that can help you to be more assertive when you need to be.

You don't like to rock the boat. Conflict, especially one-on-one confrontation, is very difficult for you. You need to feel the support of your manager and of others in your group. You tend to let others have their way if they're very set on it. You seek solutions that are acceptable to everyone. You may give in to restore harmony even if the issues aren't resolved. While you may try to calm those who are upset, you feel powerless to do anything about the conflict. You generally become more quiet and reserved if one arises. You're caring. You're loyal. But rather than stuffing your feelings, learn techniques to be more assertive. Sometimes it's important to stand your ground.

C: Concerned and Correct

In this situation, you are careful, reflective, and reserved. You want to do things right. You like logical, systematic approaches. You want to control the factors that affect the quality of your performance. At the end of the day, you expect your hard work to be appreciated. *In this situation:*

You want to work alone in a calm, businesslike atmosphere. You would probably rather write than talk, and you probably prefer memos to chitchat. You aren't comfortable in a work environment that's informal, or loosely structured, or where socializing is expected. You don't want to share information about your personal life.

You prefer to cover all bases. You want to process information before you act. You are serious about every detail and about the overall outcome. You go over everything, then over it again, pros and cons, causes and effects. You think and rethink. No matter how hard and long you work on a project, as soon as it's done and out, you'll think of a much better way it could have been done. You worry that you won't find a fatal flaw. You might make a mistake!

You try to avoid being held accountable in situations where you have no control over the factors affecting quality. But, as for all managers, much will remain outside your control no matter

Conscientiousness Style

Motivates You
- Wanting to be right
- Logical, systematic approaches
- Rewards for quality and accuracy
- Specific feedback

Demotivates You
- Rules or expectations that change constantly
- Lack of time to process information
- Mandatory socializing
- Lack of quality controls

Your Preferred Environment
- Time and resources to attain your standards
- Reserved, businesslike, and task-oriented

You Avoid or Dislike
- Being criticized, especially when you lack control
- Lack of time to evaluate consequences
- Emotionally charged situations
- Disclosing personal information

To Be More Effective
- Become more open to other people's ways.
- When other people comment on your performance, consider that they may only be trying to help.
- Try to loosen up a bit. No one has to be right all the time.

what you do. If you were the only one baking the apple pie, you could choose the kind of apples you prefer, use white or brown sugar, pick cinnamon or nutmeg, and bake it until the crust is as dark as you like. As a manager, you have to "bake the pie" with a whole group of other people who have their own ideas.

You respond to conflict with the silent treatment. You avoid emotionally charged situations. If conflict is inevitable, at first you may become defensive. You'll probably want to withdraw, then come back with facts and logic supporting your position. If that approach fails, you may use indirect forms of aggression, such as passive resistance. You may become rigid, withhold information, or simply fail to follow through.

You are a perfectionist. It's great to have high standards, but you're probably being tough on yourself, and everyone else. Are you missing deadlines because you want to make sure that everything is exactly right? That can make you a less effective manager, and it may draw criticism. Knowing how miserable you can make yourself trying to be perfect, consider other people's feelings, as well as the facts, when you evaluate their work. Be willing to negotiate performance standards. Try to adapt, share, open up, and ask others for their opinions. You might lighten the load on your own back. No one (except maybe you) expects you to have all the answers.

DiSC Combinations
Now, if you had a combination response pattern in this situation, turn to that profile.

- DI: Active and Leading, page 125
- ID: Expressive and Involved, page 127
- DS: Self-Motivated and Helpful, page 129
- DC: Self-Reliant and Analytical, page 131
- SI: Flexible and Supportive, page 133
- IS: Encouraging and Cooperative, page 135
- IC: Tactful and Observant, page 137
- SC: Respectful and Accurate, page 139

- DIS: Comfortable and Engaged, page 139
- IDC: Confident and Determined, page 142
- DSC: Responsible and Accurate, page 144
- ISC: Responsive and Thoughtful, page 146

I'm a Manager, Not a Mind Reader

You've been using DiSC to learn about you. Now you can use this same tool to learn about the styles typically used by the people you manage. Your understanding of the DiSC dimensions will help you recognize the responses of others and discover the implications for you.

You are not a mind reader; you can't know what someone else is thinking and feeling. You can, however, read other people's behaviors. Since behaviors express the ways people are feeling and thinking, they will give you clues about what's going on inside.

DiSC helps to hone your powers of observation so you can pick up the clues. DiSC also sorts what you observe into patterns so that you can better understand others and choose the right strategies for managing them. If you were to use trial and error to learn which strategies are most effective with which people, you might get there eventually, but think of the high cost in time, money, and emotional energy. DiSC can help you save all three of these valuable resources.

As always when taking and using DiSC, keep repeating "in this situation." Like you, each person on your staff is multi-dimensional and may respond to different situations in different

ways. For example, a new hire who is showing S behaviors during her first team assignment might begin responding in an I way once she becomes comfortable with the group.

It's important not to label people ("He's an S."). Labeling is not only unfair to the person, but can lead you to choose a management approach that isn't best for the true situation before you.

Instead of oversimplifying and generalizing, use DiSC to focus on a specific situation in which you and the other person are involved. Perhaps it's a situation in which you feel comfortable or content, but it's more likely that you're feeling frustrated, confused, even angry— that's why you chose to single it out. The DiSC results can help you decide the best way to act in this situation. They can help you communicate more clearly, delegate a task, help someone make a decision, solve a problem, increase motivation, recognize high performance, or correct underperformance.

DiSC can help you make effective management choices. It can also help clear any tensions or misunderstandings that are surrounding this situation.

Introducing Others to DiSC

The best way to find out someone else's response style is to ask him or her to take the tool and share the results. If you're excited about what you're learning, pass it on!

Ideally, everybody you work with will take DiSC and use the results. A group understanding of DiSC can foster cooperation, acceptance, and trust—the keys to top performance in today's increasingly diverse and team-oriented workplace. Perhaps the greatest benefit is a common language for talking about feelings, thoughts, and behavior. This language is objective and nonjudgmental. It describes what is, not what should be. DiSC can help your group communicate better and focus on issues, rather than on "personality conflicts."

If you'd like to go about this with some professional guidance, you can contact Inscape for a list of authorized facilitators in your area. It's probably not a good idea to play trainer if you have no experience. We recommend that you spread the word about DiSC one person at a time. Do what comes naturally. If you manage people regularly who you think would be open to this self-learning, tell them about this book.

Adults are just-in-time learners. When they need to learn something, they learn it. As the saying goes, when the student is ready, the teacher will appear. If you try to interest someone who isn't ready, you'll just frustrate yourself.

If you ask people to take DiSC, they may be worried that you're giving them a test. Explain that your goal is to become a more effective manager; this puts the emphasis and responsibility on you, not them. Assure them that there are no wrong or right answers. Promise that your aim is not to test and fix but to discover and capitalize, and make good on your promise. Be enthusiastic (even if you don't usually have an I style) about the ways you've benefited from this tool.

It would be great if everyone involved in a situation ran to their desks, took DiSC, and shared their results and new insights. But you live in the real world, so you need a way to make an informed guess of the other person's likely response in a situation. That's where people-reading comes in. People-reading is useful when you:

- manage a staff of dozens
- manage the other person infrequently or indirectly
- feel it's not appropriate to ask your boss to take DiSC
- work briefly with a freelancer
- want to better understand a client or customer

In situations like these, you may want to discern someone's style without the tool. So you read the response by observing behavior. In this chapter, you'll learn *signs that a person is using one style or another.* The signs are behaviors that you can observe. You look at *what* the person is saying and doing—and *how.*

Signs

Starting on page 41 are lists that can help you make an educated guess at the style with which someone is responding to a particular situation. Because people-reading is less exacting than the DiSC instrument, you can identify a single high dimension, but not a single, double, or triple response pattern. Though this approach can never be as accurate as taking the DiSC instrument, it can help you interpret real-life management situations.

As always with DiSC, begin by choosing a focus and writing it down. Hold the focus in your mind while using the tool. Pick a situation in which you are managing the person. Observe:

- how the person is communicating with you
- how the person is working with you and others in the situation
- how the person is approaching the task, problem, or change

When reflecting on a situation, you may want to make a copy of the lists and circle everything that applies. Then look for patterns and clusters in your observations. You probably will not check off every item under one style. For one thing, not all the items may be relevant. For example, in a business-as-usual situation, you won't be able to observe how the person reacts to change. Also, since everyone is multidimensional, the person's behaviors are reflecting varying levels of all four dimensions, and several dimensions may be high.

Despite the limitations, the lists can heighten your awareness of the other person's behaviors. For now, focus on the other person's behavior, not on how you are feeling about it. If you are frustrated or angry, set your feelings aside. You might imagine you have hired yourself as a consultant to observe the situation: You are someone who is impartial, unprejudiced, and lacking any stake in the outcome. Later, you should definitely bring yourself back into the picture, but first take a solo portrait of the other person. It's human nature to pay the most attention to ourselves, not others. It's valuable to shift your focus to the other person involved in this situation. Think of it as an out-of-body experience.

In addition to considering the items in the lists, ask the two questions that underlie the DiSC dimensions: Does the behavior seem typical of someone who finds the situation favorable or not favorable? Does the behavior seem typical of someone who thinks he or she can control or change the situation, or someone who doesn't?

Whatever your conclusions, remember that they apply only to this focus situation. In a different situation, the same person may respond with a different DiSC style, so don't fall into the labeling trap.

Signs of the D Style

When communicating, the person is:
- loud
- decisive
- interrupting
- direct
- restless
- formal
- inquisitive
- sometimes blunt

When working with you or others, the person:
- tends to take charge
- wants to make the rules
- asks to work independently
- may lack patience
- is competitive

When approaching a task, problem, or change, the person:
- asks questions starting with "what"
- is goal-oriented
- looks for problems to solve
- initiates changes
- is determined

Signs of the I Style

When communicating, the person is:

- outgoing
- friendly
- enthusiastic
- casual
- persuasive
- charming

When working with you or others, the person:

- seems to enjoy collaborating and is good at it
- builds consensus
- gets people excited
- recruits others for a project

When approaching a task, problem, or change, the person:

- asks questions starting with "who"
- asks to work with others
- introduces new ideas
- is okay with changes that need to be made—as long as others are on board

Signs of the S Style

When communicating, the person is:
- quiet
- tactful
- friendly
- casual

When working with you or others, the person:
- is sensitive to the other person's needs
- expresses concern for the other person's well-being
- demonstrates patience
- appears easygoing

When approaching a task, problem, or change, the person:
- asks questions starting with "how"
- wants to work with others
- offers ideas
- prefers to follow rather than lead
- is good at identifying problems
- seems uncomfortable with change

Signs of the C Style

When communicating, the person is:
- cautious
- reserved
- private
- formal

When working with you or others, the person:
- may prefer to work solo
- may grow impatient

When approaching a task, problem, or change, the person:
- asks questions starting with "why"
- wants to get the project organized
- likes structure
- keeps an eye on details
- wants things done right
- spots problems
- takes responsibility
- wants to keep things the way they are

Expanding to 4 Dimensions

DiSC helps you gather information about a situation and everyone involved in it, but you decide how you will use that information:

1. Choosing to do nothing at this time
2. Managing the situation with your first-dimensional style
3. Adapting your managing style to meet the needs of the situation

Each option would demand more of you than the one before it but potentially has greater rewards. The results may be worth the extra effort. It may not be possible to resolve a situation without going to the next level. Sometimes, though, the best choice is to do nothing at all. Start by considering the first option, and work down the list until you reach the level that seems right for the situation.

Choosing to Do Nothing

Consciously choosing to do nothing is a form of taking action. It is not the same as just ignoring the situation. Ask yourself three questions:

1. Is this situation important to me?
2. Is it possible to change this situation?
3. If it is possible to change this situation, are the potential rewards worth the effort?

You will not be able to manage everything that happens around you, nor should you. Your hours, energy, and resources may be better spent elsewhere. Later, as the situation evolves, you may decide to take action, so keep an open mind.

Before you stop at the first option, consider the possible consequences of not acting. If there is tension in your working relationship, will you begin to avoid the person? Will you tiptoe around, being overly polite and cautious? Do you tend to wait until the tension really builds up and then explode? Do you hide your feelings but feel quietly resentful?

Consider whether it would be more effective, and less stressful for you, to take some small action now. Many times, a small change will make a big difference.

Using Your First Dimension

If you choose to act, next consider the second option: managing the situation with your natural response style. This option has two advantages: You work from your greatest strengths, and you get to stay in your comfort zone.

Reread the profile of your highest dimension and of your response pattern, this time looking for assets you can bring to a situation. Aside from DiSC, you also have skills, knowledge, and experience that can help you to manage this situation.

When you feel it is appropriate and comfortable, you can choose to share what you have learned about yourself and the situation by completing the instrument. Your DiSC knowledge can help you to express your feelings and thoughts clearly. DiSC provides a vocabulary of objective, positive words that can help everyone gain clarity and emotional distance.

You can improve many situations by giving those you work with a heads-up concerning areas in which you don't feel comfortable. Let others know what pushes your buttons. They'll know better what to expect from you, and they may take certain responses less personally.

When you are in a managing role, in some situations it will be appropriate to ask the other person to adapt to *your* needs and wishes—or at least to meet you halfway. Others may not realize what's important to you. If you want people to bottom-line reports for you, you should let them know. If you need details, tell them.

Some managers have formalized this process by giving people who work for them some written "guidelines." One named her list "6 Things You Should Know about Me." This might have seemed dictatorial, except that she also asked each person for his or her own list. This created a two-way street for sharing information.

Another manager (who tended to have a C response) created a list for herself on a note card. She called it "What I Need" and taped it in a private place inside her desk drawer. It reminded her of information she needed to share with the people she managed, for example, "Remind them that you want to see all the data."

When explaining your style to someone, be clear. What's "direct" to you might seem "rude" to someone who has a different high DiSC dimension. Examples are useful.

Remember that there are no bad styles. Each dimension has many strengths, and some of these may be just what the situation requires.

Liz, the highly regarded principal of a large suburban high school, used her D style very effectively. Every day, she managed dozens of situations involving teachers, staff, students, and parents. Her days were filled with tricky situations in which quick decisions were needed. When there were student behavior or safety issues, people needed to leave her office with a clear resolution.

Usually, Liz could stay within her style and get good results. Staying in her style didn't mean she hadn't stretched and used other dimensions when appropriate; her work sometimes called for attention to details, or supportiveness, or enthusiasm. Liz was also aware of the possible limitations of her style, and she worked at listening, getting input, being patient, and expressing opinions less bluntly. However, she would describe herself as direct and decisive: as a person who responds with D. She didn't try to be

somebody she wasn't. To others, she appeared genuine and comfortable with herself, and she was widely respected and liked within the school community.

You are going to be most effective and comfortable when
working from your natural, first-dimensional style, so stay "at
home" when you can.

Adapting Your Managing Style

The third option is to move beyond your first dimension and
adapt your management style to get the results you want.
Adapting means using a different response to meet the needs
of a situation. This is moving from 1-dimensional managing
to 4-dimensional managing. Adapting is not an attempt to
change who you are, but a practical solution for a specific
situation.

Before you can adapt effectively, you need to understand
what's really going on in the situation. People tend to carry a lot
of assumptions around. You need to check yours against reality,
by using DiSC.

What Adapting Looks Like

Cassandra had recently been promoted to head nurse for a
pediatric clinic. She now supervised ten nurses. It was late
spring, and the clinic was experiencing its annual deluge of
health forms for camps and summer sports. Cassandra knew
there had to be a better way to manage the flood, and she also
knew she didn't have time to develop it. She decided to ask one
of her nurses, Bruce, to set up an efficient process for the
clinic to schedule camp and school checkups and complete the
forms.

Cassandra called Bruce into her office. "Here's what you need
to do," she told him. She handed him an outline and directions
on how to organize the work.

Bruce had been excited when first told he was going to take
on this new project, but the feeling went away as Cassandra went
over the list point by point. Some ideas had immediately popped
into his head, but when he tried to share them, she wasn't interested. After ten minutes, Bruce had become frustrated. "Look," he
said, "I think we're going about this all wrong."

Cassandra was stunned. She said, a bit sarcastically, "What's *your* big idea, then?"

To her surprise, Bruce had many big ideas. Most of them made a lot of sense, as it turned out he had done scheduling in a previous job.

Bruce grew more animated as he explained his ideas. Cassandra, who was impressed, said, "I'll give you until Friday, but I have to see an implementation plan by then."

She had the plan the next day, and it was very good. The office sailed through the busy time, and both patients and staff liked the new system.

Cassandra was happy with the results, but she stuck with her usual approach to delegating. Sometimes it seemed to work, sometimes not. By chance, her hospital was offering workshops for new managers, and she signed up. At one of the workshops, she took DiSC. She chose as her focus situation the meeting with Bruce. She realized that she had delegated the work in a C way by providing a detailed, systematic plan. This would have worked well with some of the nurses, but as she learned about the other styles, she thought that Bruce was using the D dimension of behavior. She could see this in how direct Bruce had been in trying to make her hear his ideas and in how he wanted to create the plan his way. Cassandra had switched her approach during the meeting— she'd adapted, though she hadn't been happy about it at the time. She told Bruce to devise the plan his own way and report back to her. When given the responsibility and the authority, Bruce had put an excellent plan in place. Bruce needed to be given the big picture, then freed from control and supervision.

Cassandra realized that her willingness to adapt had made all the difference.

Moving Out of Your Comfort Zone

Does adapting seem weak to you? It's actually the opposite. By adapting, you are taking action. Does adapting mean bending over backward for the people you manage? You do consider their needs, but you also consider your needs and those of the organization.

Even a small amount of adapting can feel uncomfortable. The different style may be new to you, and it may trigger concerns.

Each of the four dimensions tends to be associated with a specific concern:

- A person responding with D tends to fear loss of control, which can make it uncomfortable to empower others in the situation.
- A person responding with I tends to be afraid of social rejection, which can make it uncomfortable to confront others.
- A person responding with S tends to be afraid of sudden change and personal rejection. Both fears make it uncomfortable to create change, which makes the situation unstable while raising the possibility that people won't like what you have done.
- A person responding with C tends to fear criticism, which makes it uncomfortable to risk being wrong.

Don't be embarrassed about these concerns. *They are there because of your strengths!* For example, if you tend to respond with the C dimension, you produce accurate, high-quality work. No wonder it would make you uncomfortable to flex in a way that might let errors creep into the project.

When assessing a situation, be honest with yourself about your fears. Think about whether they are valid. Have you been in a similar situation with this person before? What risks are involved in adapting, and what is the potential gain?

Tips for Adapting

Adapting stretches you. As with stretching your muscles, stretching your style gets easier the more you do it. You become more flexible, and you can stretch further and more comfortably.

If adapting seems too much of a stretch right now, here are some tips that can help you get started. These ideas have helped other managers develop this valuable skill.

- Often you don't need to change *what* you do, just *how* you do it.
- Start small. Often even a small amount of adapting can make a big difference. Take baby steps.
- Start with a low-stakes, low-risk situation, not a full-blown crisis.

- Start with a situation that is going fairly well, but could be even better.
- Often you can get very valuable information simply by asking the other person, "What's important to you in this situation?" The answer will help you identify the kind of adapting that will make the most difference. Other good questions are "How can I help?" and "How do you see this situation?"
- Ask for feedback on whether the adapting is working for the other person. For example, when delegating, you could ask, "Does this feel like the right amount of information, or do you want more or less?"
- Afterward, reflect on the results. Did adapting work out the way you expected? What might you do differently next time?

Once you've tried adapting and it's worked, you'll feel more comfortable doing it next time.

Remember that you won't always have to adapt. You will continue to use your first dimension in many situations.

Are you worried that the other person will see the adapting as manipulation? This is unlikely. The other person may experience your adaptation several ways, depending on your primary style and his or hers. The person may feel grateful, respected, understood, thanked, valued, or reassured.

Don't be surprised if the other person responds by adapting to you. If you take a small step toward someone, that person often will take a small step toward you—or even a giant step. The person may see that you're making an effort, and that can do a lot to ease tension and build a relationship. Don't assume that you will be the only person willing and able to work on this relationship.

Above all, think baby steps.

Not a Fix-All

So far, we've been talking about the many ways that DiSC can help you understand and improve management situations. DiSC is a great tool. However, like all tools, it can't fix everything that's broken.

If you have both been working from your strongest dimension and adapting your style, and the situation is still stuck, consider whether this situation requires other strategies.

Using DiSC will provide you with the ability to understand differing points of view on the same situation. Sometimes, such differences aren't the root of a conflict. Other possible causes include the following:

- different values (when someone believes a deeply held principle, like fairness, has been violated)
- unclear expectations
- lack of resources (insufficient staffing, a scarcity mentality, inadequate funding)
- lack of job skills or experience
- organizational change and transition
- lack of shared goals or purposes
- unpopular but necessary managerial actions (need to keep information confidential, legal requirements, orders from above)

Even in these cases, though, DiSC can help build mutual understanding and defuse surrounding emotions.

Using DiSC Day to Day

You have a wide range of options—all the way from choosing to do nothing to adapting. Depending on the scope and importance of the situation, you may choose an option after just a moment's reflection, but try to discipline yourself to take that time.

You might spend a few quiet minutes, or take a brisk walk, reflecting on your options. Many people find it useful to write their thoughts down, particularly if the situation is unfamiliar or complex. Some people are doodlers; some people need to talk things over with a trusted colleague or someone at home. You may want to guide your reflections with one of the action plans at the end of this chapter or in later chapters.

You may be asking, "When am I supposed to find the time for all this?" Consider the time of reflection as an investment. Spending a few minutes now can save you hours and hours down the road. There will be fewer derailed projects. Fewer tasks you thought were delegated will become your responsibility again. Employee turnover will probably be lower, too—think of all the time saved training new hires.

Day in and day out, using DiSC takes very little time. Once you are familiar with the four basic styles, you can start using DiSC as situations develop in front of you. You are certainly not expected to sit down and take the instrument every time a situation arises. After all, you might be managing many people and situations every day.

It is a good idea to consider taking the instrument more formally when you're up against a complex or intractable situation. Have you and someone become like gasoline and fire? Is your department facing a big change?

After you apply DiSC, think about the results. What worked? What didn't work? What would you do next time?

The more you use DiSC, the more instinctive and powerful it will become for you. The following chapters will get you started. First comes an introduction to using the four dimensions in the basic managerial tasks: coaching and communicating. Following are chapters on everyday responsibilities like delegating and giving feedback. You will learn how to start putting DiSC to work.

Managing the Situation

➤ What is my natural DiSC response to this situation?

➤ Who else is involved in this situation? How is this person responding? (Or how do you think he or she will respond?)

➤ What are the primary needs of the situation (include your goals, the organization's expectations, the staff person's preferences)?

➤ Options (Read all, then circle one.)
   1. Do I want to take action at all? In other words, is changing the situation worth it to me?
   2. Do I want to respond to the situation in my natural, usual way? What strengths would this bring to the situation?
   3. Do I want to adapt my management style to meet the needs of the situation? If so, how? What concerns would I have?

➤ Specific actions I will take with this person (include what, when, and how):

➤ Implement the plan and consider the results. What did you learn about this person? How can you be more effective with him or her in the future? What follow-up is appropriate?

Basics of 4-Dimensional Managing

Let's look at the challenges and opportunities that you are likely to have when someone you manage is responding with a particular high dimension. Depending on your own response to this situation, you will find some of the suggestions natural and comfortable, and others a stretch. Whatever your own response style, you have strengths on which you can draw to meet the needs of this person and your situation. There will also be many opportunities to adapt.

Managing D

People with a D response often do their best work when allowed to do things their own way. They want to manage themselves, so how do you manage them and their work? If you want their respect, you need to be direct and confident in expressing your expectations. Be self-assured and clear in your dealings with them. You don't want to butt heads, like two rams in a nature film, so show respect in addition to strength and use tact.

If experience suggests that these people are capable of producing excellent results their own way, you often will manage best by giving your support and a lot of room. If things aren't going well, step in only until the project gets back on track. It isn't effective to micromanage these people who respond in a D way.

These people want control of the situation and will grab it from you or anyone else. Here's a common scenario. Leah has taken over a project that was assigned to Dan and his committee. She stepped in because she thought the project would benefit from her expertise but has become so "helpful" that she's taken over. Even if she's doing a fine job, she's in somebody else's space. Tell her she's in the wrong pasture but that her skills are greatly needed in her own backyard. Oh, and if she has extra time, you'd like to talk with her about an exciting new project that's just come up.

How to Communicate

Stick to the facts. Skip the small talk and get right to the point. Deliver a straight, clear message in as few words as possible.

Watch for selective hearing. People responding with D tend to hear and remember only what they agree with. When you're talking, watch for signs that the person's mind has wandered. Pull your listener back into the conversation by asking for an opinion.

Use the power of the written word. Another cure for selective hearing is to arrive at a meeting with a succinct outline or an agenda. They'll admire the efficiency, and you'll have a paper trail in case amnesia develops.

Ask for a solution to a problem. Listen to ideas and give them thoughtful consideration. A person responding in a D style is more likely to buy into a solution if it's his or hers. Explain which ideas you like before pointing out any flaws in the thinking. Be aware that some of the implications and details of a plan may have been overlooked.

How to Coach

First, close the door. This person hates to lose face. When you give feedback, be private, positive, and firm. Keep your voice matter-of-fact. At the same time, keep it strong, so there's no doubt who's in control. Maintain steady eye contact. Don't let yourself be bulldozed.

Focus on specifics. You won't get results with either general direction (which will be ignored) or indirect criticism (which will be resented). Focus on the goal and specific obstacles to achieving it.

Sell the usefulness of others. D behavior is great for pushing people to action, but it can come across as uncaring, demanding, even autocratic. You can help this person and the whole group by pointing out how others are being affected. Underscore, again and again, how important co-workers can be to one's success.

Managing I

What's the best way to channel all that enthusiasm and optimism? Call on these people when the group needs an infusion of positive energy. Ask them to help you win support for a new procedure or a change. Invite them to brainstorming sessions. Build variety and flexibility into the assignments.

Their people skills can be a great asset to you. They connect well with others, draw them out, and can win them over. They know everyone and nearly everything about them.

They are highly motivated by social recognition. When they have done particularly well, announce it at a departmental meeting, at a recognition event, or in the company newsletter.

Respond to their enthusiasm with matching energy, and they'll be eager to go along with you.

How to Communicate

Listen. They love to talk about anything and everything. It's easy to engage them in lively, open-ended, freewheeling conversation. They like to talk so much, in fact, that they probably interrupt all the time. They really, really want you to listen to what they have to say.

Ask them to lunch. When you want to talk things over, choose a friendly, relaxing, informal setting. Allow enough time to share a few stories, experiences, and ideas.

Check in frequently. They "don't sweat the small stuff," so you have to stay on top of the situation. Too often, your directions are muddled or even forgotten. People responding with high I find details unimportant. You'd better put priorities, check-in dates, and deadlines in writing, and check back often.

Ask what, when, where, how. These questions will help translate big ideas into realistic plans. Ask them as often as possible. If necessary, follow one with another: "What do you expect to do?" "How do you intend to do it?" "When will it be completed?"

Watch the time. Meetings with these people may go on too long. They can't help it—they could talk all day long! Before you begin a meeting, use the old trick of saying that you have to be somewhere at such and such a time.

Clarify what was decided. At the end of a discussion, ask for a summary of what was decided, to make sure everything was heard and understood. Review both the main points and key details.

How to Coach
Keep it private. This person's worst nightmare is to be criticized in front of someone else—or worse yet, in front of a group. Instead, talk over any problems in private.

Improve follow-through. The person responding in an I style has a big weakness—lack of follow-through. Projects are started full of fire, but the inevitable details, procedures, and complications smother the flames. Ultimately, he or she needs self-discipline, but your coaching can help. When the implementation phase becomes boring, even painful, you can feed the fire with your own enthusiasm and with recognition for jobs well done.

Managing S
Relaxed, friendly, cooperative, and patient, these people want to help you. They don't want to lead—they want you to lead them. So be clear about your expectations, and don't throw surprises at them.

Relationships are important to these people. At first, they'll be nice enough, but reserved. Give them as much one-on-one time as you can spare, so they can become comfortable. Show that you are open to ideas and that you like them and their work. Once you've built a strong relationship, these people are likely to be loyal to you.

How to Communicate

Chat. It's pleasant and comfortable to chat with people who have a strong I dimension. They show great tact and sensitivity with you and others. You might set up regular, informal, casual discussions. A relaxing coffee break might work.

Ask for input. They are so supportive, so easy to get along with, that you might think they will just go along with everything. In fact, when there's a problem, they want to offer their ideas before decisions are made. But you'll probably have to ask.

Keep the lines open. When there's a problem, they don't speak up. They don't want to stir up trouble. They'll follow through with whatever you ask, but they may be suffering inside. They'll go to all lengths to avoid confrontation. Take time to draw out their thoughts and feelings about the situation. It often helps to share your own thoughts first. They need to feel they are standing on safe ground. Express how much you appreciate the many times they help you and how you want to repay that loyalty by helping when you can.

Pay attention. Listen not just to what the person says, but also to the tone of voice, body language, and whole style of behavior. Here's an example. Peggy, an obstetrical nurse, came in to work late one morning. She'd assisted with a couple of difficult deliveries during the night and had had only a little sleep. Her face was grim, and her posture sagged. Still, when her co-workers greeted her with the usual, "Hi, Peggy. How are you?" she answered with the customary, "Fine."

"How can you say that?" the desk nurse asked. "Weren't you here most of the night?"

Peggy turned her head back and snapped, "Do you know what 'fine' really means? It's Frustrated, Insecure, Neurotic, and Exhausted." She'd been pushed over the edge.

How to Coach

Build confidence. The S style of behavior is overly modest. This is a major limitation. These people can be more effective if they project more self-esteem. Your coaching should include lots of expressions of appreciation for their fine skills and accomplishments.

Overcome fear of change. They crave stability. Change—especially sudden, unpredictable change—is a big problem for them. When introducing a change—big or small—talk about it in a calm, logical way. Work together to develop a step-by-step plan, with checkpoints and a final due date. Encourage them to ask questions, both right away and later on as they occur to them.

Managing C

They analyze every decision and direction. Getting it done isn't the goal; getting it perfect is. They'll do it over and over again, never finishing until you push them to move forward.

When you assign a task, give them as much background and detail as possible. Try to build in time for a reasonable amount of research and thought.

Often their insights will be worth the time spent. However, people who respond with high C can slow the group down as they examine every angle. There are times when this is essential, and times when it's not necessary or helpful. Make it clear which is which.

How to Communicate

Don't do lunch. Business lunches drive these people crazy. Can a person possibly accomplish anything serious and eat at the same time? It is far better to meet in a businesslike atmosphere like your office or a conference room. Meet one-on-one and explain what to bring along. For a team meeting, have a written agenda.

Get right to business. State the purpose for your meeting up front; then go over the topics in a logical, systematic manner.

Don't start with small talk about the football score, the weather, or your kids. It would make them uncomfortable and antsy.

Be precise. As you talk, try to use precise language. John and Dave have two mutual friends both named Roger. Whenever John says to Dave, "I talked to Roger today and . . ." Dave always interrupts his story right there and asks, "Which Roger?"

John said, "I bite my tongue every time because I want to blurt out, 'If you keep listening, in about two words you'll figure it out,' but he can't listen any further until he knows 'which Roger.'"

Communicating Up

Reading the styles of your boss and other upper managers can help you choose the best way to communicate information to them.

- When presenting information to someone who responds with D, get right to the point and keep it brief. When possible, save this person from too many meetings by offering to give the bottom line afterward. Also, don't keep interrupting every time something comes up; take things as far as you can on your own, and save the rest for one discussion.
- When presenting to a person showing the I style, meet face-to-face, and leave lots of time. This person wants the high concepts and big ideas, not reams of facts and figures. Follow up with a brief summary of the decisions that were made and the next steps.
- Respond to an S-style person's request for input on a project even if you think it's a waste of time—this person wants inclusion and consensus.
- A person who tends to respond with C prefers to receive information and reports in writing, and in detail. For the best reception, if your boss worries over every detail, don't greet him or her with problems first thing in the morning. Give this person time to settle into the day's routines first.

This need for clarity is typical of a C conversational style. These people tend to be precise in communications, which sometimes makes others feel as though they talk down to them.

How to Coach

Focus on the issues. The major limitation of the C style is a tendency to be overly critical of themselves and other people. They hold themselves and others to very high standards. This can be hard on everybody. Others may find them demanding and irritating, and soon C-style people will find that they are alone and burnt out. When coaching, give detailed, specific feedback in an unemotional way. Focus on issues, not on the emotions surrounding them. Help keep the big picture in focus, and gain some perspective on the project and everyone's role in it.

Speak out! They need to become more comfortable in emotionally charged situations. This won't come by shielding them. Even though they may work best alone, make sure they also are involved in decision-making meetings and encourage them to contribute. Ask for their opinions on things you know they feel strongly about. They need practice confronting people directly, rather than with indirect gibes.

4-Dimensional Delegating

CHAPTER SEVEN

WORK WITH ME
- **D: CONSIDER ME ON THE JOB.**
- **I: I'D LOVE TO WORK WITH YOU ON THAT!**
- **S: I WILL HELP YOU WHEREVER POSSIBLE.**
- **C: I ONLY HOPE THAT I CAN DO IT TO YOUR STANDARDS.**

Many managers hesitate before they delegate. They're worried that the other person won't do the job as well as they could themselves. So they keep for themselves some tasks that could have been done by others.

This hesitation is perfectly natural. As a manager, though, you need to get work accomplished through others. Delegating helps you get more done, and allows you to take advantage of other people's strengths. When you hold back from delegating, you aren't doing your job. You will cut into the time you have for your other responsibilities, and you won't have time for new, more interesting assignments. You may have to rush through your work, failing to meet your own standards. You may burn yourself out, trying to do your job as well as other people's jobs.

When you don't delegate, you can also hurt the people you manage. Someone misses out on an opportunity to learn, grow, or be recognized for good work. You need a skilled, effective staff that can get the job done. On a purely self-serving level, you're more likely to be promoted if you have groomed someone to take your place.

Let's go back to the number one reason why managers don't delegate: They are worried that the person won't do the job as well as they could themselves. The manager thinks the person is not able or willing to do a good job. Perhaps there have been times when the person turned in poor results—sloppy, late, incomplete, or just wrong. Perhaps the manager had to step in and take back the assignment.

Depending on your style, there are other reasons why you might not delegate:

- If you are having a high-D response, you may not want to lose control of the situation.
- If you are having a high-I response, you may have trouble structuring an assignment or just may be putting it off.
- If you are having a high-S response, you may feel uncomfortable with the leadership aspects of delegating.
- If you are having a high-C response, you are probably worried that the other person will not meet your high standards; even if you do delegate, you will probably keep working independently, keeping others in the dark.

You may hesitate because you think the other person lacks the required skills or because you think the person lacks interest or motivation to do the job right. In either of these cases, you may want to explore ways that, as the manager, you can help develop skills or improve attitudes.

Consider, though, that at least part of the problem may be the way you are delegating. You may be having problems delegating if:

- Projects are too often finished past deadline.
- Directions seem to be treated lightly, even ignored.
- You're continually interrupted to explain the process again.
- Staff complains about lack of cooperation from others in completing a task.
- Individuals decide to go off on a tangent, doing it their own way.

- Projects are delayed until the last minute, forcing a rushed, unsatisfactory finish.
- You have way too much on your plate.

You may be thinking, "But my way of delegating works just fine with the person who used to have that job. This new person just doesn't get it." This is a case of two different people responding to the same situation in two different ways—in fact, with two different DiSC dimensions.

Your delegating style may work just fine for many people, but when it isn't working, consider how you might choose to adapt to the needs of this situation. There are D, I, S, and C ways to delegate. Read the style of the other person, and think about the best way to delegate to him or her.

First, consider whether the person is right for this job. Perhaps another staff member would be more comfortable and do better with this particular assignment. On the other hand, perhaps the person will be able to stretch and grow through this assignment.

When choosing to whom you'll delegate something, it's important to separate competency from behavioral styles. A person might have the required skills and knowledge, but not be the best choice for this task. On the other hand, you don't have limitless people working for you. You might have to delegate to somebody because the task falls in his or her area of responsibility. Perhaps you need to delegate to the person who has the time to take on the task. If the skills or experience are not quite there, you may need to help someone develop new competencies. It's not unusual for a manager to act as a teacher, trainer, or coach in developing the staff. Here again, behavioral styles come into play. You can structure the learning experience to be done in the way the person will best understand and absorb.

For example, Tiffany, who had an I style, seemed to be a good choice to be the spokesperson for a local United Way, but she had no media experience. Her manager decided that this important responsibility merited some investment in coaching for Tiffany. His first thought was to hand her a couple of good books on the subject—that's how he himself often picked up new skills. But after thinking about Tiffany's I style, he realized that this approach wouldn't work as well for Tiffany. She would learn better in an environment that included discussion and dialogue. She'd want to ask lots of questions and even role-play. He found a dynamic, high-energy media coach who brought Tiffany up to speed in no time.

You can also use DiSC to determine the amount and type of information to communicate when delegating. For example, some people need detailed, step-by-step instructions. Others want to know the desired result and the deadline. Looking ahead, DiSC results can help you plan how you will follow up and supervise the work. The right delegating style will help you get the results you want.

The person to whom you delegate may still get to those results differently than you would have. It's usually a mistake to force someone to do things your way. The person can become frustrated or resentful and may not be able to achieve good outcomes. On the other hand, it's always a mistake to be unclear about your expectations. If very high quality is your priority, say so. If the deadline is firm, say so. If the most important thing is creative solutions, say so. Share the organization's priorities, too. What results does your boss expect? Give the person the bigger picture.

Here are some things to think about when delegating to a person who tends to have a D, I, S, or C response.

Delegating to D
- Be very clear about the desired results.
- Give a deadline.
- Clarify the limits of this person's authority and the available resources.
- Let this person determine how to get it done and work independently.

If you tell a high D what results are needed and why, you can feel confident that he or she will come through. A high D will figure out how to get the job done and do it. Stay in the loop though. Check in from time to time to make sure that things are still on track.

Delegating to I
- Make sure this person understands the results that you expect.

- Be firm about the time frame for completion.
- Set dates for checkpoints with a clear understanding of what is to be completed by each date.
- Help structure a process for completing the task, especially when dealing with a complex task or an assignment that requires a methodical approach.

The biggest challenge for a person responding with I is self-discipline. This person can easily get carried away with new ideas and lose sight of the original assignment.

When you find yourself managing a high I, make sure expectations are understood. Make sure the person has a plan, particularly if the project is complex or calls for a methodical approach.

Delegating to S

- Provide a step-by-step explanation of what is required, with written documentation whenever possible.
- Be available for regular follow-ups and to handle questions.
- Clarify the resources available for completing the assignment.
- Help gain cooperation from others where necessary.

This person wants you to spell it all out. A high-S person is dependable once you've explained and double-checked every detail of the assignment but will be hesitant to do one thing without a map. This person doesn't want the responsibility. If you tend to respond as a high D, you may be frustrated if you delegate what seems to be a simple task, only to find the job partially done and to hear, "Oh, I didn't know you wanted me to do that, too."

Delegating to C

- Provide a logical, accurate, precise description of what you expect, including standards of quality.
- Explain why the assignment is being done and how it fits in with the overall operation.
- Be firm about the deadline.

Unless you are clear on the results and timeline, this person may get lost in overanalysis and overresearching.

State exactly what you want, both aloud and on paper, because this person will go over and over your instructions and follow them exactly. Unless you've explained in detail the bigger picture, this person may build a marine park for a goldfish.

A high-C person is not a clock-watcher. You may have to tell this worker when it's time to stop. If you've outlined the job on paper, ask that every detail be checked off as it is finished. Give an earlier deadline than is necessary, then call "Time!" when the real deadline arrives.

The job may not require perfection, but you'll get perfection. Ringing in this worker's head is the thought, *"What if I make a mistake?!"* Make it clear that the biggest mistake that can be made is to accomplish little or nothing in the time allowed; that if too much time is spent warming up, the race is lost.

Delegating

D: Consider me on the job.

- Tell them the ultimate goal, but let them determine how to accomplish it.
- Be clear about deadlines and available resources.
- Outline the limits of their authority.
- Let them work independently.

I: I'd love to work with you on that!

- Clearly define the results that you expect.
- Set firm deadlines.
- Enforce a project schedule.
- Help them complete complex tasks by structuring a methodical process for each assignment.

S: I will help you wherever possible.

- Offer a step-by-step explanation of what is required.
- Be prepared for frequent meetings to evaluate progress and to answer questions.
- Clearly outline the resources that are available.
- Help them recruit the assistance of other employees.

C: I only hope that I can do it to your standards.

- Provide a detailed explanation of the task.
- Stress standards of quality and accuracy.
- Explain the purpose of the assignment and how it will benefit the organization.
- Set clear deadlines.

Delegating

> Describe a situation in which you want to delegate a task:

> Is the person likely to respond to this in a D, I, S, or C way?

> What style do I usually use when delegating to others (D, I, S, or C)?

> What is needed in this situation to make the delegation successful?

> What aspects of the person's response to delegated tasks should I support and encourage?

> What aspects may cause problems, and how can I address them?

> Should I use my natural response in this situation or choose to adapt?

> What action will I take and when?

4-Dimensional Decision-Making

Once upon a time, managers were all-powerful people who sat behind big desks. They made decisions. They told people what to do and how to do it.

This doesn't work today, and hasn't for some time. Organizations have become less autocratic and more participatory. This is part of a shift from pyramid-shaped, top-down, vertical organizational structures to flatter, horizontal structures. Organizations still have managers, and they still give their managers responsibilities and goals. The big difference is that the people being managed have substantive responsibilities and goals, too. Today, most organizations expect people on all levels to make decisions, either individually or in teams. As a result, it has become important for managers to help the people on their staffs make sound decisions.

71

A sound decision is one that has been appropriately researched and well analyzed. It is timely, widely accepted, and leads to good results. Clearly, decision-making is a complex skill, one in which many of your staff members will lack experience or confidence. Common shortcomings include the following:

- rushing to make a decision
- making impulsive decisions
- relying too much on intuition and hunches
- failing to get input from others
- moving ahead before a decision is made
- taking too much time to reach a decision
- overdoing the research and analysis
- shying away from decisions that may be unpopular

You can use your knowledge of DiSC to help individuals on your staff make the most of their decision-making strengths and overcome their decision-making limitations. Your coaching can help people make decisions that are good for you, for them, and for the organization.

Decision-Making with D

People responding with the D dimension want to make decisions quickly.

- Point out the benefits of taking time to gather enough information and to consider possible consequences before deciding.
- Encourage the involvement of others when decisions will affect them.
- Clarify who has the authority to make which decisions.
- Ask to be informed of decisions that are made.

These people make fast decisions because they are confident about their knowledge and judgment, and because they are comfortable with a high level of risk and are willing to accept that not every decision will turn out right.

On the positive side, decisions get made. On the negative side, you may not always like the decisions. If you can help them to develop the patience and processes to make wiser decisions, the outcomes will be better more often.

Point out that if they want to rise in the organization, they have to be seen as people who can be counted on to make good decisions.

Jon was given the responsibility of getting new photographs for a product catalog. For the first time, the company was going to publish its catalog in both paper and online versions. Jon, who responded to this task in a D way, immediately called up the same photographer the company had used in the past. He wanted to get the job done, and he didn't think it was necessary to get quotes from other vendors.

When Jon told his manager that he'd scheduled the photo shoot, the manager asked whom else he had considered. When he heard nobody, the manager directed Jon to get two other quotes before moving ahead. "Okay," said Jon, "but it won't be my fault if this deadline goes bye-bye."

Three days later, Jon had to report that, to his surprise, both photographers he'd contacted had given much lower estimates. Plus, one of them specialized in digital photography, which was critical for the new online catalog.

Sometimes, jumping to conclusions can mean jumping past opportunities to do things better.

Decision-Making with I

People responding with the I dimension tend to base decisions on intuition rather than facts and to avoid making decisions that may be unpopular or controversial.

- Talk about the ways that good decisions, popular or not, will ultimately benefit the enterprise and the decision-maker's reputation.
- Point out that indecisiveness may frustrate others and look bad.
- Help develop a more logical, fact-based approach to decisions.

There are times when a tough decision must be made, and not everybody will be happy with the outcome. This is when a person who makes decisions in a high-I way will need your coaching the most. Watch especially for a tendency to leave every difficult decision up to a group vote.

The high-I decision-making style is based too much on gut feelings and not enough on facts. If a decision seems to have been made too quickly, send the person back to reconsider it. Sometimes, playing the devil's advocate is necessary; this person may be overly optimistic that everything will turn out right in the end.

Be aware that whatever the two of you decide today, the decision may be reversed innocently tomorrow for "a better idea." A decision should be a decision.

Decision-Making with S
People responding with the S dimension need time to think things through.

- Support this methodical, logical approach to decisions that have an element of risk.
- Identify decisions that should be made more quickly because they are less important or carry less risk.
- Give extra support when the decision involves potential conflict.

Sarah was losing patience with Kimberly, the manager of a bank branch. Sarah was vice president of human resources for the main office and often worked with Kimberly on staffing issues. "Whatever I suggested, she would say, 'Yes, yes, whatever you want me to do,'" Sarah complained. Kimberly had good judgment and years of experience, yet demurred whenever there was a decision to be made.

One fall, the bank was making staff layoffs. Kimberly would have to make the cuts at her office. Tough decisions had to be made. It was Sarah's job to tell each branch manager the number of positions to be terminated, but it was Kimberly's job to decide whom to lay off.

At the meeting, Sarah gave Kimberly the big picture, explaining that without the cuts, local branches like hers would have to be closed. Sarah also coached Kimberly on how to deliver the bad news. Sarah said she was confident that Kimberly would make fair and wise decisions—and she did.

With direction and support, a high-S person can make excellent decisions that take into consideration the facts, the people involved, and the organization's expectations. However, decision-making will be uncomfortable when it involves risk, change, or conflict, which is where your positive support can help.

A high-S decision-maker wants to be fair to everyone involved. That's an admirable goal, but it isn't always possible. Again, your understanding and support can help.

Decision-Making with C

People responding with the C dimension tend to approach decision-making analytically, calculating risks and potential payoffs.

- Allow enough time to gather information.
- Discuss how much time should be spent in project analysis.
- Set a time limit for a decision.
- Step in if the process gets bogged down in "what if."
- Be reassuring about personal consequences of being wrong.

The C decision-making style is to get all the facts, check and recheck them, and look at pros and cons. Sometimes that's what is needed. Other times, the process delays decisions that need to be made so that work can move ahead.

Encourage them to keep looking at the big picture. Advise them to prioritize along the way and to keep due dates in mind.

If they become overwhelmed contemplating possible outcomes, offer your assistance. Remind them that there's a forest, not just lone trees.

Suggest that they ask themselves:

- How long do I have to make this decision—six days or six months?
- What are the risks involved?
- What results do I want?
- Which battles should I fight and which are wastes of energy?

Decision-Making

D: Let's make this decision quickly.

➤ Encourage them to take the time to gather information and evaluate potential consequences.
➤ Ask them to consult others who will be affected.
➤ Clarify who will make certain decisions.
➤ Stay informed about decisions that are made.

I: Let's get everyone involved in this decision.

➤ Discuss how indecision will frustrate others and affect interpersonal relations.
➤ Encourage the use of logic and information.

S: I think you should make the decision.

➤ Capitalize on their methodical decision-making strategies in situations with an element of risk.
➤ Encourage them to make decisions more quickly in situations with minimal risk.
➤ Support them when they make decisions that will receive resistance from others.

C: I'd like to spend some time researching the situation.

➤ Give them time to gather the facts.
➤ Set a time limit for analysis and enforce deadlines.
➤ Give perspective on the true consequences of being wrong.

Decision-Making

➤ Describe the situation about which a decision will be made:

➤ Is the person responding (or likely to respond) to the decision in a D, I, S, or C way?

➤ How do I usually make decisions like this one (D, I, S, or C)?

➤ What is needed in this situation to make a good decision?

➤ Which aspects of the person's decision-making style should I support and encourage?

➤ Which aspects may cause problems, and how can I address them?

➤ What action will I take and when?

4-Dimensional Problem-Solving

As long as there is work, there will be problems, big and small. It is worth spending time to help your staff become more effective problem-solvers, because problems they can't solve will become your problems.

When a problem comes up, some people analyze the facts and systematically work toward a solution. Others listen to their intuition. Some people tackle a problem right away. Others ignore it and hope it will go away.

People respond to problems, as they do to other situations, in a D, I, S, or C way. Sometimes the natural response works well. For example, if the problem calls for intense scrutiny and extensive research, a C approach will yield great results. Other times, though, the natural response is not effective. The process or the outcome is not what it might have been.

Someone you manage is having trouble with problem-solving if he or she is:

- ignoring important details
- not taking time to study the problem
- solving a problem over and over, never being satisfied with the results
- avoiding problems whenever possible
- trying to solve everything without checking with you first

If the problem and the person are totally unsuited to each other, you may want to assign this challenge to someone else. Usually, though, the problem will stay where it is, and you'll work with the person already involved in it. Your DiSC knowledge can help you draw on the person's natural strengths in solving problems, as well as help the person to adapt and approach the problem in a new way.

Some problems are directly related to people's high dimensions. That isn't true of all problems, of course. Whatever the cause of the problem, as soon as someone tries to solve it, his or her DiSC style becomes part of the picture.

Problem-Solving with D

Steve, who was in charge of the pressroom for a printer, was outgoing and ambitious. He wanted to make things happen. He would never knowingly let a mistake get past him. The problem was that he rushed, especially once he had things moving along. So mistakes were happening much too often. His manager had talked to him about these problems in the past, but they were still occurring.

Then the manager decided that rather than telling Steve what to do, he'd lay out the problem and ask Steve to figure out how he could reduce the number of errors in his department. The manager gave him the big picture—the messed-up orders, the customer complaints—then gave him a deadline for reporting back with a plan. As always, Steve threw himself into the challenge—and this time, because the solutions were his, they stuck.

When you problem-solve with someone using a D style:

* Challenge him or her to find the solution.
* Strongly recommend that complex problems be handled more slowly and in greater detail.
* Take a practical, results-oriented approach.
* Look for simple, easy-to-implement, immediate solutions.
* Put the problem in a wider context.

Problem-Solving with I

These optimistic people see few problems. They are not prone to sweating the small stuff. They want to avoid open conflicts, too. However, their people skills, keen intuition, positive energy, and contagious enthusiasm can help the group resolve many tricky problems.

Steph was a copywriter at an advertising agency. To get the creative juices flowing, she liked to play music, and she'd even run old movies on the VCR in her office. The other members of the creative team would gather in her office, and they'd laugh and throw out ideas while tossing around stuffed animals or spongy balls. The problem was that the accounting department was next door. Steph's circus atmosphere was driving them crazy.

Her manager decided to ask *her* how to reconcile the problem of disturbing other departments. She immediately asked, "Could we make a 'creative zone' in the back corner of the warehouse—with lots of room to spread out and do whatever we want, without bothering anybody?" The brainstorming session yielded several other possible solutions, too. The manager then coached Steph to talk to the rest of the people and gather more ideas. Whatever the plan, he was sure that Steph's enthusiasm would quickly win over the others.

When you problem-solve with someone using an I style:

* Value the person's gut feelings and good insights into people and situations.
* Coach the person not to stop there, but to follow through and analyze the problem.

- Help the person develop new problem-solving skills, such as breaking the solution down into steps.
- Encourage the person not to ignore problems that involve conflict or are complex.

Problem-Solving with S

The goal of S-style problem-solving is to find a solution that is acceptable to everyone. These people listen carefully and consider the needs of others. This approach can yield solutions that work well and are widely accepted.

When conflict arises and people don't agree on a solution, S-style people tend to give in to restore harmony, even if the issues aren't resolved. People problems are often ignored altogether.

It's difficult for S-style problem-solvers to take the lead. Tell them you and the group need their help, though, and they may rise to the occasion.

People and their feelings rank high with Marsha. Too high? She was always missing deadlines because she'd gone out for a long lunch with someone who was having a rough day, or spent hours listening to somebody's woes. Marsha's manager decided to ask to talk about the wonderful service she'd been providing to the others. He gave her a verbal pat on the back for her regard for others. Then he pointed out how much work time she'd used up listening to personal problems, while her assignments were only half done. He asked for her help. Marsha was a sensitive soul and became concerned about the organization's dilemma. Once the manager made his expectations clear, she went overboard trying to make things right.

When you problem-solve with someone using an S style:

- Value the step-by-step, methodical approach to solving problems.
- Coach the person to develop innovative solutions when the usual ones won't work.
- Allow enough time to study problems before asking for a solution.
- Give direction in determining which problems require extensive study and which require immediate action.

Problem-Solving with C

It seems strange, but you will sometimes have to coach people who solve problems in a C way not to be so thorough! They won't run away from problems—they're always looking for them. As great detectives, they'll find problems, but sometimes they need to pick up the pace.

Arlo, an overly conscientious order fulfiller, was a gem, but he was costing the organization clients. His manager shared the bigger picture with him, pointing out that speedy delivery was necessary to compete in their market. She asked Arlo to investigate (thoroughly, of course) the effectiveness of other ways of checking orders. Arlo worked for days and days researching the latest software for order fulfillment. The manager checked in from time to time to see how things were going, and she set a deadline. On the day of the deadline, Arlo handed in a report that recommended investing in some custom software. When installed, the software speeded up the whole department's work while reducing errors.

When you problem-solve with someone using a C style:

- Value the analytical, systematic approach to solving problems.
- Be aware that this person will want to find the perfect solution. Suggest alternative problem-solving techniques for problems that need more immediate solutions.

MANAGER'S CHECKLIST
Problem-Solving

D: Let's find a quick solution.
- Express confidence in their ability to find a solution.
- Encourage them to examine complex problems from all angles.
- Define the expected results.
- Look for practical, easily implemented solutions.

I: I know just how we can solve this problem by working together.
- Compliment their insight into people and situations.
- Emphasize the need to go beyond instinct and analyze the facts.
- Divide the process into steps.

S: I need to think about the problem before I can offer you a solution.
- Compliment their methodical problem-solving.
- Encourage them to use innovation and creativity.
- Give time to reflect before asking for a solution.
- Help them evaluate the urgency of problems.

C: I'm going to consider this problem from every angle.
- Compliment their analytical abilities.
- Offer perspective when they want a "perfect" solution.
- Outline alternative problem-solving techniques for situations that require immediate decisions.

MY ACTION PLAN
Problem-Solving

➤ What is the problem?

➤ Is the person responding to this problem in a D, I, S, or C way?

➤ How am I responding to this problem (D, I, S, or C)?

➤ What is needed to solve this problem?

➤ Which aspects of the person's response to problem-solving should I support and encourage?

➤ Which aspects may cause problems, and how can I address them?

4-Dimensional Motivating

CHAPTER TEN

WORK WITH ME

- **D: CHALLENGE ME.**
- **I: GET ME INVOLVED.**
- **S: SHOW ME HOW I CAN HELP.**
- **C: GIVE ME TIME TO DO THINGS RIGHT.**

You can lead a horse to water, but you can't make it drink. Unless, of course, it's thirsty. Then you'll have a hard time pulling it away. We're all motivated to do what we want to do.

Let's say your group has been charged with launching a new product. You call a planning meeting. Someone proposes starting with a weekend retreat for brainstorming. Most people respond enthusiastically to the idea, finding it extremely motivating. A few people, though, look stunned. They want to go into their offices, close their doors, and get to work alone. An idea that is highly motivating to some is off-putting to others.

To motivate literally means to put in motion. We feel motivated when something attracts, entices, or inspires us. That "thing that moves us" is not always easy to put into words. It's easy to sense, though, when motivation is lacking in someone. Here are some of the trouble signs:

- stalling
- resentment
- stale thinking
- poor work
- absenteeism
- withdrawal

If someone is acting like this, motivation is low. Ultimately, no one can motivate someone else. People motivate themselves. We are all motivated by what we want to do, by the needs we want to meet—not by someone else's wants and needs. You *can* help create an environment in which someone will feel more motivated.

Your DiSC knowledge can help. People feel motivated when their work environment is meeting their needs. Each DiSC response pattern is associated with certain needs, and so each pattern is related to certain motivating factors.

People responding with the D dimension feel motivated to achieve, while those responding with the I dimension are motivated to seek social recognition. People responding with the S dimension feel motivated to keep things the same, and people with a high C feel motivated to make sure things are done correctly.

If you would like someone to feel more motivated, these are the questions to ask:

- For a person showing each particular DiSC behavior, how many motivating factors are in the current work environment?
- If there are not enough, how might you take steps to meet more of the person's needs?
- What demotivating factors are in this person's work environment?
- How might you eliminate some of them?

You asked similar questions about yourself as you explored your own response pattern. The sections below repeat the "motivating factors" and "demotivating factors" from chapter 3, so you can consider them in the context of managing others.

Motivating D

This person is motivated by:

* control of the work environment
* directing other people's activities
* new opportunities and challenges
* opportunities for advancement

This person feels less motivated when he or she:

* is being questioned or overruled
* has limited responsibility for results, people, or situations
* has only restricted access to resources
* is under close supervision

To increase motivation:

* Provide opportunities for independent work.
* Increase the person's control over the work environment.
* Assign responsibility for directing others.
* Create competitions and chances to win.
* Provide opportunities for advancement.
* Reward success.

This person will feel motivated when there is a chance to achieve. A highly motivated, high-D person will drive toward a goal, making it happen. If achievement will bring advancement, this person will leap over the top bar.

When Margery Hurst left the British army after World War II, she discovered that her husband had deserted her and her two little girls, and she had no way to support the family. She was angry, and she had something to prove. She rented a tiny room and a phone and put out a sign that read "TYPISTS AVAILABLE." Whenever the phone rang, she would briskly say, "I'll send over one of my best women right now." Then she would lock up the room and go to the job. Gradually, the calls came so often that she began to hire her girlfriends to go out, too. This was the beginning of Brooke Street Bureau, the first temporary service agency, which later became a worldwide company.

Ms. Hurst was motivated by the need to achieve. She didn't mind the risks, and she kept plugging away until she was successful. She liked doing things her way.

Let people with this style know what you want; then let them go ahead on their own as much as possible. If these people are too closely supervised or expected to make frequent reports on each step along the way, motivation will fall. Instead, make the goal clear, and let them figure out how to get there.

Motivating I

This person is motivated by:

- dialogue with others
- immediate verbal feedback
- enthusiastic recognition
- acknowledgment of feelings

This person feels less motivated when he or she:

- encounters reserved or unfriendly co-workers
- is restricted by rigid schedules
- faces pessimism
- has to perform routine, detailed tasks

To increase motivation:

- Structure assignments so the person can work with a group.
- Listen to his or her thoughts, feelings, and ideas.
- Recognize achievement enthusiastically and publicly.

If the organization focuses on facts to the exclusion of feelings, people with this style will lose altitude fast. People are their world. If co-workers are nasty, unfriendly, or reserved, people with a high-I style feel down.

Fixed schedules and rigid time constraints may be unbearable. Don't put a butterfly in a box. They need room for expression and for the unexpected. Allow this, and motivation will probably rise. If some routine, detailed tasks are necessary, try to structure the job so they can do them with others. Be sure to stop by often to give compliments on progress.

A person with this style would probably feel highly motivated if put in charge of facilitating a team, planning a party, or emceeing an event. These are good outlets.

Several months after her husband died, Gracie knew that she wanted to be around people. She was not about to sit at home alone and be depressed. At age sixty-five, she persuaded a high-end supermarket store that they needed someone to be a hostess/nutritionist. It was an original idea. Although she had no special training for the job, her enthusiasm and sparkling personality won them over. For many years, she drove more than sixty miles from her little town to the big city. Not a blizzard, broken leg, or sickness held her back. When you walked into the store, Gracie would meet you with her joke of the day (always a good one). She would remember your birthday, help you plan your shopping, scold you if you bought high-calorie foods, and help you plan special diets. Everyone loved Gracie because she was friendship and laughter.

She defined the job and it paid off handsomely for the store in both customer goodwill and employee relations. People came to the store just to shop with Gracie.

Her motivation? Being with people and spreading good cheer.

Motivating S

This person is motivated by:

- cooperating with others
- clearly defined responsibility and authority
- providing good service
- job security

This person feels less motivated when he or she experiences:

- rapid, unpredictable change
- competitiveness and aggressiveness
- lack of support from managers or co-workers
- one-on-one confrontation

To increase motivation:

- Provide opportunities to work cooperatively with others.
- Make your expectations very clear.
- Thank the person for helping.
- Reward consistent, predictable performance.

A nurse became angry when she observed what she saw as malpractice in the delivery room. She thought some medical practices were causing injuries to babies and mothers. When she complained to her supervisor, she was told, "Well, why don't *you* do something about it?"

She did. Her first move was to enroll in law school, where she graduated with honors. Now, many years later, she is a nationally recognized lawyer who champions unborn and newly born babies and their mothers. Respected in both the medical and law fields, she sits on review boards in both professions. Wherever she sees what she believes is an injustice in this area, she gives her all to make things right. What motivates her is helping babies and mothers. Her supervisor's remark woke her up to the fact that she could do something about this.

Someone who is responding with S behavior can be found heading up the United Way campaign or collecting money for flowers for a co-worker who's in the hospital.

What is the motivation? People with this style want to help others. All you have to do is ask. A person responding as a high S wants to know what you need. Be clear about the parameters of the job and the specifics of tasks you assign. This person finds it motivating to know what you need and how you want it done.

Motivating C
This person is motivated by:

- wanting to be right
- logical, systematic approaches
- rewards for quality and accuracy
- specific feedback

This person feels less motivated when:

- rules or expectations change constantly without explanation
- there isn't time to process information
- socializing is mandatory
- quality controls are lacking

To increase motivation:

- Create opportunities for demonstrating expertise.
- Support efforts at creating quality results.
- Provide situations in which logical, systematic effort will contribute to long-term success.

Why sweat blood if no one notices or cares? People with this behavior style can lose their edge and eventually become angry. If you let them know, privately and sincerely, how much you appreciate their results, they'll knock themselves out.

They tend to feel motivated if they can work intensively and alone. Even in a team-structured work environment, you may be able to find some projects on which they can fly solo for a time.

The costume designer for *Gone With the Wind* spent enormous time and effort creating the petticoats of Scarlett O'Hara's maid, Hattie. They had to be made of a fabric that would rustle so Scarlet could hear that Hattie was eavesdropping. The details of the period costumes had to be just perfect, too. Most movie productions have people working and reworking minute details behind the scenes. Their motivation? Getting things right.

Motivating

D: Challenge me.

- ▷ Provide opportunities for independent work.
- ▷ Increase the person's control over the work environment.
- ▷ Assign responsibility for directing others.
- ▷ Create competitions and chances to win.
- ▷ Provide opportunities for advancement.
- ▷ Reward success.

I: Get me involved.

- ▷ Structure assignments to allow teamwork.
- ▷ Listen to their thoughts, feelings, and ideas.
- ▷ Recognize achievement enthusiastically and publicly.

S: Show me how I can help.

- ▷ Provide opportunities to work cooperatively with others to achieve tangible results.
- ▷ Make your expectations clear.
- ▷ Recognize their contributions.
- ▷ Reward consistent performance.

C: Give me time to do things right.

- ▷ Create opportunities for demonstrating expertise.
- ▷ Support efforts at creating quality results.
- ▷ Provide situations in which logical, systematic effort will contribute to long-term success.

MY ACTION PLAN

Motivating

➤ Is the person responding in a D, I, S, or C way?

➤ What are the signs that this person is not feeling motivated?

➤ Review the motivating factors for the person's response style. Which are part of his or her current work environment?

➤ If there are not enough motivating factors, how might I take steps to meet more of the person's needs?

➤ Review the demotivating factors. Which are in the work environment?

➤ How might I eliminate some of them?

➤ What actions will I take and when?

4-Dimensional Complimenting

- **D: OF COURSE YOU APPRECI-ATE MY EFFORTS—I DID A GREAT JOB!**
- **I: OF COURSE YOU APPRECI-ATE ME—EVERYONE KNOWS I DID A GREAT JOB!**
- **S: I'M GLAD YOU WERE PLEASED WITH MY PERFOR-MANCE.**
- **C: IT'S GOOD TO SEE THAT HARD WORK IS VALUED AROUND HERE.**

Paying someone a compliment is like giving a gift. When you buy a present, you begin by asking yourself, "I wonder what this person would like to get?" When you give a compliment, it's a good idea to ask the same question.

Everyone has a friend or relative who always gives presents that would be great for him or her, but are all wrong for the recipient, like the uncle who gives everybody the latest thriller because that's what *he* likes to read. Even kids catch on to this. Six-year-old Lori told her mother, "I know what Kevin will bring me for my party. Legos. Legos are his favorite, so he always gives Legos."

DiSC can help you discern the kind of recognition that someone other than you is likely to be happy to receive. What will the individual see as a true compliment? What will be accepted? What will be treasured?

People feel most genuinely valued when they receive recognition for personal characteristics that they consider strengths in themselves or others. Someone with an Influence style probably would not consider being called analytical a compliment. A person with a C style probably *would* feel complimented by being called analytical. In fact, one person's compliment can be another person's insult.

The way you give a compliment matters, too. A person responding with an I style wants to be praised in front of others, while a person responding with a C style would rather have it in writing, or at least in private.

Think about how you like to be recognized. That's probably the way you are most likely to compliment others. Sometimes that will fit the other person's idea of a good compliment, sometimes not—and you may choose to adapt your style to meet the needs of the situation.

Managers who tend to have a D style often forget that recognition is important to many people. The manager of a large division said, "I don't need a lot of praise. I know when I've done a good job. I started to notice some time ago, though, that lots of people keep complimenting me. I used to think this was just a snow job. It was irritating. Now I see that they do it because *they* really need praise and I'm neglecting them. The way they keep

AT THE OSCARS

WHEN SOMEONE IS HANDED THE MOVIE BUSINESS'S HIGHEST COMPLIMENT AT THE ACADEMY AWARDS:

- **A D RESPONSE IS TO DESCRIBE HIS OR HER ACHIEVEMENT, BUT STAY WELL WITHIN THE TIME LIMIT.**

- **AN I RESPONSE IS TO BE IN HEAVEN (THINK OF SALLY FIELD'S GUSHING, "YOU LIKE ME, YOU REALLY LIKE ME.").**

- **AN S RESPONSE IS TO THANK EVERYONE WHO HELPED WITH THE FILM.**

- **A C RESPONSE IS TO READ FROM A PREPARED STATEMENT, TO BE SURE NOT TO MISS ANYONE WHO SHOULD BE THANKED.**

praising me is the clue." If you are a high-D manager, consider that recognition can be a powerful tool to help you achieve your goals. Parents find that when they praise a behavior, the child is likely to act that way again. In fact, their praise is remembered far longer than their scolding. Your staff is more mature than little children (at least on most days), but they still will find your compliments motivating. A well-chosen, well-delivered compliment is a powerful management tool.

Complimenting D

- Keep it brief and direct.
- Focus on specific achievements and results.
- Praise leadership abilities.
- Don't play games; make sure the recognition is deserved.
- Don't get mushy.

They want to be recognized for tangible things and for achieving big results, not for every step or nuance along the way. "We couldn't have done it without you" is a compliment they'll cherish for a long time.

When you deliver a compliment, keep it to a sentence or two, and don't go overboard. They won't respect you if they think you're trying to butter them up.

Complimenting I

- Do it publicly.
- Be enthusiastic.
- Compliment verbal ability, interpersonal skills, and creativity.

Compliment them often and publicly. Make it fun, a clever presentation, if you can. If your organization has a lot of people who respond with this style but has no formal recognition programs, consider starting one. While they like the gushing, it's still important to be specific about what is being praised.

Complimenting S

- Be warm and sincere.
- Express appreciation for cooperation, supportiveness, consistency, or loyalty.

Compliments are important to people who are responding with S behavior. They give them to others, and they need to hear them. Like people of other response styles, these people want to be recognized for qualities that they value most, in this case cooperativeness and loyalty.

Complimenting C

- Do it in private.
- Be brief and specific.
- Sometimes, put it in writing.
- Be accurate.
- Recognize logic, competence, precision, and hard work.

They want to know that you noticed and appreciated how much time, energy, and smarts they put in to the task to make it come out exceptionally well. They are serious about this, and they can spot fake flattery and will resent it. They would like you to be specific with compliments. Mention every detail you can, but briefly, and they'll look forward to their next opportunity. Ignore their efforts, and they'll be crushed.

Ask them if they have any suggestions about how the team could become more efficient. Ask which resources would help them to do their jobs. Asking them for advice tells them they are the experts. It's a fine compliment.

TRUE COMPLIMENTS

- **TO D: "YOU SAW WHAT NEEDED TO BE DONE, AND YOU DID IT."**

- **TO I: "YOU ARE SO GREAT—YOU AMAZE ME."**

- **TO S: "I REALLY APPRECIATE THE WAY YOU FOLLOWED THROUGH AND KEPT AT IT UNTIL THE JOB WAS DONE."**

- **TO C: "I REALLY APPRECIATE THAT YOU MADE US LOOK AT ALL THE PROS AND CONS, BECAUSE THE DECISION WE MADE WON'T COME BACK TO BITE US."**

MANAGER'S CHECKLIST
Complimenting

D: Of course you appreciate my efforts—I did a great job!
- Be brief and direct.
- Focus on specific achievements and results.
- Praise leadership abilities.
- Offer only sincere compliments.
- Avoid emotional comments.

I: Of course you appreciate me—everyone knows I did a great job!
- Compliment publicly.
- Be enthusiastic.
- Make a point of recognizing interpersonal skills and creativity.

S: I'm glad you were pleased with my performance.
- Be warm and sincere.
- Express appreciation for cooperation, supportiveness, consistency, or loyalty.

C: It's good to see that hard work is valued around here.
- Compliment in private.
- Be brief and specific.
- Put it in writing.
- Recognize logic, competence, precision, and hard work.

Complimenting

➤ Does this person seem to respond to complimenting in a D, I, S, or C way?

➤ For what achievement or quality would this person like to be complimented, because it's something he or she values?

➤ What is the best style for giving this compliment?

➤ How do I like to be complimented (D, I, S, or C)?

➤ How might I choose to adapt my style to meet the way this person likes to be complimented?

➤ What action will I take and when?

4-Dimensional Feedback

Most people don't enjoy criticizing others, and no one likes to be criticized. People try to take the edge off criticism by calling it constructive feedback, but it can still hurt.

Still, it's part of a manager's job to help people close the gaps between current and expected performance.

Constructive feedback is meant to be just that—*constructive.* Done well, it helps to build good results. Though we too often think of getting feedback as a negative experience, its goals are positive. It gives people a chance to do better and become more successful.

While no one loves to be criticized, some people are more open to feedback than others. There are also differences among people in the things they feel defensive about. People tend to feel most threatened when criticized for falling short in an area they think they're good at—especially when it's an area that they think is important.

DiSC can help you anticipate how an individual is likely to respond to a type of feedback. You can then choose to give the feedback in a way that will lead to positive results. What you have to say will probably not change, but how you say it may change a lot. DiSC can help you give feedback that will be understood, accepted, and effective.

Giving Feedback to D

- Be direct about the desired result and the current level of performance.
- Ask the person to work out a plan for closing the performance gap, then bring it to you.
- Define time limits for improvements and clearly state consequences.

Brace yourself for these common D responses to corrective feedback: ignoring you, blaming others, expressing anger or resentment, and attacking. Come ready for action.

Be strong. At the same time, show appropriate respect for the person's abilities. Give the person as much responsibility as possible for bringing performance in line with expectations.

Use a clear, calm, direct communication style.

Giving Feedback to I

- Clearly state the performance problem and consequences, resisting any attempts to sidestep the problem.
- Focus on actions that can improve performance.
- Sell the rewards of improvement, including the chance to look good in the eyes of others.
- Schedule enough time for a good discussion, but don't allow the conversation to drift to other people and other situations.
- End the discussion by getting a commitment to a specific result by a specific time.

People responding with I behavior are experts at morphing one topic into another. Keep the discussion on topic, or you may soon find that the two of you are discussing last year's company picnic or Arnie's bad habit of not turning off the lights when he's last one out.

Also try to keep the discussion straightforward. An expressive, outgoing person may respond emotionally. To prevent this kind of escalation, keep your tone firm and measured, yet positive.

People with this response style are often weak on follow-through. Make some suggestions to get the person started toward improving the situation.

This person is more likely to accept and act on your feedback if you focus on the positive. Paint a picture of what the good results could be, and be enthusiastic about his or her ability to rise to the challenge.

Giving Feedback to S

- Recognize both the need for improvement and areas of good performance.
- Be clear about your expectations.
- Work with the person to create a step-by-step plan.
- Provide regular feedback on gradual improvements in performance.
- Use a warm and reassuring style.

People responding with the S style tend to be afraid of personal rejection, so be clear that you are criticizing the performance, not the person. Effective feedback might take the form of: "I am so glad to have you on my team. There's this one thing, though, that I'd like you to work on."

Your continued encouragement will be much appreciated.

Giving Feedback to C

- Expect defensiveness.
- Stick to a specific, factual discussion about the current results and necessary improvements.
- Give the person time to form a plan for improvement.
- Agree on a time frame, including a final deadline and points for formally reviewing progress.

The greatest fear is to be wrong. Corrective feedback says, in essence, "You are wrong." The person typically responds by denying the problem, blaming others or the situation, feeling embarrassed, or flooding the manager with data showing there's no problem.

State the needed change; then give the person time to think about the situation and develop a strategy. During the initial meeting, set a date to get back together and commit to a specific course of action. Set firm deadlines.

Giving Feedback

D: What do you mean I need to improve?

- Be specific about their current performance and about what you require.
- Ask them to create an improvement plan and set up a meeting to discuss it.
- Clarify the consequences of unsatisfactory performance and define a time frame for improvement.

I: But everyone says I'm doing a great job!

- Be direct about the performance problem and its consequences.
- Allow enough discussion time, but remain focused.
- Commit to a deadline for specific improvement.

S: Am I doing anything right?

- Recognize areas of good performance first.
- Define your expectations clearly.
- Help them create a detailed plan for improvement.
- Provide feedback regularly.
- Be warm and reassuring.

C: So if my way is wrong, then how is it supposed to be done?

- Be prepared for a defensive reaction.
- Stick to the facts.
- Give them enough time to formulate a plan.
- Agree on a formal review process and a timeline.

MY ACTION PLAN

Giving Feedback

➤ What feedback do I need to give?

➤ Does this person seem to respond to correction in a D, I, S, or C way?

➤ How should I give the feedback so that it will be understood and accepted?

➤ What kind of plan for improvement will be most effective?

➤ When and how should I follow up?

Managing in 4 Styles of Organizations

Each management situation is a triangle. At the first angle of the triangle is you. At the second angle is the person you are managing. At the third angle is a group we haven't talked about yet—a very powerful group. At the third angle is your organization.

An organization responds to things that happen within it and to it. In fact, organizational responses are similar to D, I, S, and C responses of individuals.

An organization reveals its style in the way it treats people and approaches tasks. You probably know ahead of time how your organization will react to a problem. You also know the atmosphere of the place. Is there a hush in the halls, or do you hear the buzz of conversation, punctuated with bursts of loud laughter? Is the air charged with competition, or are things friendly and relaxed?

When Peg looked at her organization, she found several indications of its style. She was a manager for a health organization that helped people overcome chemical dependency. The organization had been a pioneer in its field. Fifty years earlier, its new approaches had been very successful, and the organization had dedicated itself over the years to maintaining the principles on which it had been founded. It valued stability and continuity. Many employees had worked there for more than twenty-five years—in fact, it was an inside joke that a person had to die before a position would open up. The staff was incredibly loyal. The top managers of the organization believed in building consensus. They involved everyone in decisions and held long meetings to explain and discuss projects. Often the focus was not on the content of the ideas on the table, but the surrounding emotions and feelings. Peg would describe the atmosphere as relaxed, stable, harmonious, and pleasant. This was an S-style organization.

You can't sit your organization down and ask it to take DiSC. Even if you did, the results would not be meaningful—organizational style is not just an average of the styles of all the people who work there. But just as you learned to read other people's styles by observing their behavior, you can read the style of your work environment.

The Sources of Organizational Style

Although an organization's style is not an average of its employees' styles, it is likely to reflect the most common style of its upper management. Often the organization's founder first set the tone. An organization tends to hire people who respond as it does. Those people feel they "fit in," and they stay. Over time, the percentage of employees with the same style grows. In fact, the organization may get itself in trouble if it loses a balance of people who respond in a variety of ways.

If the organization is thriving, its style is working well, at least for now. Going deeper, it's interesting to think about why it's working. The reasons are often tied to the type of industry. GM's style works for its purpose, but its style wouldn't work at a small nonprofit agency. An insurance company will do things differently than an advertising agency, and that is a good thing. So one source of organizational style is the nature of the business.

Location, size, and age are other influences. A big corporate law firm in New York City is likely to have a different style than a small firm in a county seat in Nebraska. Also, a start-up will probably have a style different from a stable firm that has endured for decades.

All of these ingredients go into the pot, simmer awhile, and produce organizational style. The resulting dish will taste delicious to some people. These people, who have the same high dimension as the organization, feel right at home. They understand why things are done a certain way. To other people, the organizational stew seems too strong, spicy, sweet, or salty (in other terms, too D, I, S, or C). They feel like strangers in a strange land. The environment makes them uncomfortable. DiSC can help them understand what's going on around them and the ways they might choose to act so they can thrive there.

Within large organizations, a department may have a different style from the company as a whole. For example, marketing may have a different style than accounting. You can choose to examine these micro-organizational styles, too.

Reading Your Organization's Style

Answering three questions will help you discern your organization's prominent style. Take three sheets of paper (or pages in a computer file). Write one of these revealing questions at the top of each page:

- In my organization, which behaviors are modeled?
- In my organization, which behaviors are rewarded?
- In my organization, which behaviors are criticized?

Look at what the organization does, not just what it says. For example, some organization say they value risk-taking, then punish people who take risks and fail. Is it lip service or reality?

Now focus on several situations within the organization. As you did before when you took DiSC, re-create a situation in your mind. Who was there, what was said, how did people act? Jot down phrases and words that come to mind. Situations involving a change tend to be especially revealing, so you might want to include your organization's response to a new procedure, a new product line, a merger, or a restructuring. Include at least one situation about people and at least one about tasks. As with people reading, look only at behaviors; don't try to guess what people are thinking or feeling.

After you have at least ten words or phrases on each page, look for patterns in your responses. Then read the lists on pages 114 and 115 looking for matches. Write D, I, S, or C next to items in your lists that seem characteristic of that style. What style is your organization?

The D Organization

More companies today are high-D than any other style. They are hard-driving, competitive places. At the top of a high-D organization, a single person is often steering the boat. The organization is reflecting that person's vision, ideas, and values.

The organization demands results. Because time is not being "wasted" on people issues, a high-D organization often steps on people's feelings. This can be a stressful environment with high turnover and crisis management. All drive and push, a high-D organization needs help with both people and tasks. Who is taking care of the details? Who is caring for people's spirits?

Still, *a high-D company gets things done*. It gets the big contracts. With the right management, it will continue to grow.

The I Organization

In an I organization, there are lots of meetings, gatherings, and conversations. Topics are discussed at length. People share what's on their minds. There are recognition programs, banquets, awards, and great parties.

There is often competition within the organization to be creative or come up with The Big Idea. The constant need to be "on" can burn people out, leading to high turnover.

Weak on planning, structure, and details, the organization often finds it difficult to turn its good ideas into results.

Influencing organizations are often led by enthusiastic, charismatic people. Many of them were founded by someone with a new idea or product. If enthusiasm or innovation begins to fade, the organization's leaders will worry they are getting stale. One or two may leave to form another company. Thus the

Influence style does not lead to the most stable organizational structure. Still, a high-I organization can be an exciting, fun place to work.

The S Organization

An S organization is stable, harmonious, consistent, and predictable. The atmosphere is pleasant and relaxed. This organization honors teamwork, cooperation, and joint projects. It discourages heroics and strong individualism. Customers or clients drawn to an S organization will receive red-carpet treatment and find themselves working *with* the team.

An S organization tends to help its workers develop their skills. It usually reaches out to the wider community through sponsorship of charities. Its employees are loyal and tend to stay a long time.

The organization is stable—perhaps too much so. Rules and theories can outlive their purposes; 1975 problem-solving methods yield 1975 answers, not the answers needed today. If this organization doesn't dare to take a risk now and then, if it doesn't update its goals and procedures, it may be pushed out of business.

The C Organization

The hallmarks of a C organization are quality, accuracy, and order. This is a careful company that prides itself on producing perfect products and results. Research is presented with pie charts, bar graphs, and reams of paper. There is a place for everything, and everything is in its place.

Punctual, idealistic, hardworking, dependable employees are valued. Consistent, excellent results are rewarded. The atmosphere is businesslike. There may be a formal or informal dress code.

The high standards can take a toll on the staff. When the workload gets heavy and the hours get long, employees may suffer from stress or sleep deprivation.

The organization may miss opportunities because it spends so much time researching and analyzing. It may also resist growth, because it fears the lowering of standards.

Signs of D

Models:
- quick decisions
- competitiveness, both within itself and toward other organizations
- love of a challenge
- directness
- forcefulness

Rewards:
- independence
- winning
- decisiveness
- speed
- results
- status

Criticizes:
- softness, weakness
- nitpicking
- foot-dragging

Signs of I

Models:
- much interaction, both one-on-one and in meetings
- the importance of relationships
- expressing thoughts and feelings
- optimism
- belief that work can be fun
- constant change

Rewards:
- creativity
- enthusiasm
- passion

Criticizes:
- too much emphasis on research, rules, or regulations
- dullness
- ignoring the group
- insensitivity

Signs of S

Models:
- stability and security
- harmony
- teamwork and joint projects
- pleasant, relaxed atmosphere

Rewards:
- conformity
- cooperation
- helpfulness
- loyalty

Criticizes:
- disruptiveness
- pushiness
- going for the jugular
- strong individualism

Signs of C

Models:
- high standards
- careful analysis
- weighing of pros and cons
- tact and diplomacy

Rewards:
- accuracy
- completeness
- attention to detail
- on-time performance
- dependability

Criticizes:
- mistakes
- sloppiness
- lateness
- spotty research
- hyperbolic enthusiasm

Meeting the Organization's Needs

You've been using DiSC to discover and address your needs and the needs of the people you manage. Now you can add a third set of needs: your organization's. An organization's needs reflect its DiSC style.

- A D organization needs to achieve results.
- An I organization needs variety and recognition.
- An S organization needs stability and close relationships.
- A C organization needs accuracy and consistency.

Every organization's highest need is to meet its goals. There are many types of organizational goals. Some organizations have goals with dollar signs in front of them. Others have goals like growing, serving others, building community, or winning awards. Some organizations are very clear about their true goals while others are less focused. Your job as a manager is to help the organization reach its top goals, whatever they may be.

When your work helps the organization meet its needs and reach its goals, it will reward you. When it doesn't, you may irritate, confuse, or anger other people.

Your organization will be most comfortable when things are done its way. If your natural response to a situation is different from your organization's style, there are many ways you may bring your organization's style into your management of the situation:

- Put a spin on the way you manage something, so it's more acceptable in your organizational environment. Sell the way you handle a situation.
- Decide, in a high-profile situation, that it's politically wise to follow the company line.
- Adapt to improve the way you are perceived in the organization.

Does this mean that you don't do what you think is best in the situation? This could happen at one time or another, but for the most part, it will be enough to adjust your style slightly. It's often not what you do, but how you do it.

Your natural response style may very well provide the balance the organization needs, but don't expect it will always be well received. That doesn't mean you should change who you are. It does mean you should ask yourself these questions:

- How will my management style look to the people who are judging my performance?
- How can I help this organization perform more effectively?
- How can I use my special strengths most effectively in this organization?
- How can I better succeed in this environment?
- How can I help the people I manage succeed?
- In what areas are misunderstandings about me most likely to develop?
- Is this organization likely to give me messages of value?
- Is there a gap between what I need and what the organization needs? How might I close this gap?
- Will this organization *ever* be "right" for me—and vice versa?

For everyday decisions, you won't always have to include the organization in your thinking. But for major decisions and recurring situations, consider the bigger picture. Over time, the third angle of the triangle will have a big impact on your effectiveness and happiness.

You in This Place

Whichever behavioral style you use most often, whichever organizational environment you're in, you can succeed. However, you may face some challenges. Here is a look at how your organization's style might affect you as a manager.

In a D Organization

If you have a D style. You know what you're dealing with. Give it all you've got. Be yourself, and they'll respect you. Expect some conflicts along the way, because other people will have strong opinions, too.

If you have an I style. This can be a great match. A high-D organization will value your enthusiasm and energy. You will appreciate that your ideas are quickly implemented. However, the organization may not always recognize your great work. It just expects it.

If you have an S style. The place may feel unstable, cold, and harsh. Others may come to you for comfort and a sympathetic ear.

If you have a C style. It'll bother you that people want to push on before they look into things. And you may drive others crazy if you insist on putting on the brakes. However, the organization needs you, and it probably realizes that you help it reach its goals.

In an I Organization

If you have a D style. People working with you may share credit for your ideas. The power, prestige, and authority you want may not be there. You may become impatient in the long meetings.

If you have an I style. You may not want to go home at night because you're so pumped up to be there.

If you have an S style. The organization will embrace change faster than you will. Both you and the organization value teamwork, so you'll be pleased with the appreciation you'll receive for your work. You won't find many guidelines though, and you may long for them.

If you have a C style. It will bother you that there aren't many rules or guidelines. Realize that you're on your own when it comes to planning. Practice giving a short, quick, direct answer to each question; only you need to know the wealth of research and analysis behind your conclusions.

In an S Organization

If you have a D style. The predictable, orderly, stable environment seems dull. How did you end up here? No challenges, all these teams cramping your style. Other people will think you are rude, when you're just trying to get things done. You have two choices. One is to relax and cruise for a while. That might fit in with the rest of your life at this point. But if you are playing handball all the time to vent your frustration, consider moving on.

If you have an I style. You can trust the company and its employees. But where's the excitement? You may be just the person to spark some enthusiasm. You know how to make the place fun. You could help the others loosen up a bit. Start a rewards program for jobs well done. What can you learn from them in return? Some patience, the importance of records management, and the personal rewards of loyalty.

If you have an S style. Lucky you. You're enjoying the easygoing environment, the teamwork, the predictability of each day. What are likely to be missing are opportunities to stretch and grow. Will you be in this same position for the rest of your life? Could you be replaced? Ask for opportunities to develop special skills.

If you have a C style. You may be troubled by the relaxed standards, lack of analysis, and loosely defined performance expectations. Still, you like the consistent, predictable company style, the patient helpfulness of others. You'd like more chances to demonstrate your expertise. You'll be managing teams, so you'd better get good at it.

In a C Organization

If you have a D style. The double checking and deep analysis will frustrate you. You'll be itching to get things moving, but you'll be forced to weigh pros and cons and to calculate risks. Still, you'll know exactly where you stand at all times.

If you have an I style. You're probably bored with the repetitious assignments and continuous attention to details. Work on developing organized, systematic systems for putting your ideas into action.

If you have an S style. You'll feel at ease, but you'll probably be lonely. This organization expects you to work on your own. You like the stability of the environment, though. How much concentration are you ready to devote to details and analysis? If you aren't rigorous enough in your thinking, this organization will be critical—and you'll feel hurt.

If you have a C style. What more could you ask for? You're in a reserved, businesslike organization that values quality and dependability above all. The organization takes a systematic approach to situations and activities. Conflict is rare. You're right at home.

Managing Others in This Place

Your organization's style will affect both the effectiveness and the motivation of everyone you manage. You can help individuals succeed in this environment by drawing on their natural strengths and by encouraging them to adapt and grow. Also, if the organization is unlikely to recognize an individual's contributions, you can choose to send the right messages of value.

In a D Organization

If you're managing people who have a D style. Fight to get them juicy, high-profile projects where they can make a difference. When they are successful, recommend them for promotions and perks.

If you're managing people who have an I style. Let them know that the organization has little patience for unnecessary meetings or constant socializing. Invite them to brainstorming sessions and other creative meetings. Praise them in front of others. Coach them to apply their enthusiasm and persuasiveness toward helping the organization get the results it craves.

If you're managing people who have an S style. They won't like the independent, forceful, and competitive nature of this environment, although they will probably keep their feelings to themselves. Assure them that there's nothing personal in other people's direct, forceful comments—it's just their way. Tell them often how much you appreciate them. Nurture self-confidence.

If you're managing people who have a C style. Regularly acknowledge the excellence of their work. However, point out that a D organization puts a priority on speed. Help these people recognize the times when it's best to say "good enough" and move on.

In an I Organization

If you're managing people who have a D style. Their style is probably coming across as abrasive and antisocial. Help them work on the social skills that the organization values.

If you're managing people who have an I style. They probably love their jobs, and the organization probably loves them. Help them bloom. At the same time, encourage them to develop their follow-through and attention to detail—skills that the organization won't be modeling but which are also necessary for success.

If you're managing people who have an S style. Help them become more comfortable with the constant changes in this environment. They'll probably be too modest about their contributions. Encourage them to believe in themselves and talk them up to others.

If you're managing people who have a C style. They are an extremely careful people working in a carefree, social organization. It's a puzzling setting for them, so you may have to act as an interpreter. Encourage them to become more tolerant of others and their ways.

In an S Organization

If you're managing people who have a D style. Their tendencies toward forcefulness and competitiveness are not winning friends. They need to work on playing nice—softening their style and showing concern for others. They also will need to develop some patience, since the organization won't move fast enough to please them. Consider helping them carve out projects on which they can work alone, in their own way, and with a chance to get the glory.

If you're managing people who have an I style. Other people probably think they drink way too much caffeine. They need to tone down their energy level and tune in to the way others are feeling. Their friendliness will be an asset though, and they'll probably attract followers and admirers. You might point out opportunities to take a leadership role.

If you're managing people who have an S style. They are feeling very comfortable here. Let them know how much their cooperation and help mean to you—the rest of the organization will probably be doing the same!

If you're managing people who have a C style. They will be comfortable with the slow pace, but will probably think others are too relaxed about procedures and research. Send messages of value about their high-quality, careful work. Point out that they are probably being harder on themselves than anyone else is.

In a C Organization

If you're managing people who have a D style. Encourage them to take time to do the research and collect facts and figures before presenting ideas. Otherwise, they will not get the backing and respect they want.

If you're managing people who have an I style. They really need to develop the self-discipline to follow through on tasks. This organization won't respect their creative ideas if they can't back them with facts. Be sure to praise them in front of the group and lead a round of applause.

If you're managing people who have an S style. They'll enjoy the slow pace and stability of this environment but will find it cold and uncaring. Warm it up by recognizing the many ways they help the group.

If you're managing people who have a C style. They can research, prepare, analyze, and plan all day, and the organization will love it. Between their high standards and the organization's though, they may live in fear of criticism. Help them to gain some perspective.

BACKHANDED COMPLIMENTS

- FOR D: WHEN PEOPLE IN YOUR ORGANIZATION SAY, "HE SURE KNOWS WHAT HE WANTS," THEY MAY REALLY BE SAYING, "HE NEVER LISTENS TO ANYONE ELSE'S IDEAS."

- FOR I: WHEN THEY SAY, "SHE IS ALWAYS SO UP," THEY MAY MEAN, "SHE'S OUT OF TOUCH WITH REALITY."

- FOR S: WHEN THEY SAY, "HE IS ALWAYS SO NICE," THEY MAY BE THINKING, "WHAT A CHUMP."

- FOR C: WHEN THEY SAY, "SHE THINKS OF EVERYTHING," THEY MAY REALLY BE THINKING, "I WISH SHE WOULD GET A LIFE."

Closing Words: Going 4-Dimensional

You are a manager every time you delegate to someone, help someone make a decision or solve a problem, recognize or improve someone's performance, or motivate someone. Each of these situations has something important in common. It involves two people: you and someone else. Through DiSC, you can better understand how both of you are responding to the situation at hand—and from that understanding can come effective solutions.

You will choose how to act on what you learn through DiSC. In a particular managerial situation, do you want to draw on the strengths of your natural, first-dimensional style or use a different dimension that seems like a better approach with a particular individual? DiSC can give you insights into your managing style and the styles of the people you manage, but what you do with those insights is up to you. DiSC is a self-discovery tool and a self-applied tool.

At this point, you may be excited about 4-dimensional managing and eager to jump in. Perhaps you're already doing it. If you're ready to start now, it's a good idea to pick a situation that isn't too tense, complex, or critical. See one situation from someone else's point of view. Take a baby step and see how the other person responds. Then try another situation.

On the other hand, at this point you may recognize the potential benefits of 4-dimensional managing, but not want to change the way you work. You might think you *can't* change the way you work. No one is suggesting that you throw away your favorite managerial style. You'll continue to use your first dimension most of the time. Some of the time, though, consider whether the results you would get through adapting might be worth it.

You might start by taking DiSC a few times to help you better understand the situation and why it may be tense. Next, think about different actions you *could* take. Would some of them feel comfortable for you? Eventually, experiment and see what happens. Take it one step at a time. If you get good results, try it again.

Four-dimensional management is results-oriented. It can help improve performance and outcomes. It also lowers tension and builds productive working relationships. As you move toward 4-dimensional managing, ask yourself what's working and what isn't. Reflect on the results.

Most people who use DiSC begin by filling out the tool while focusing on a specific situation, but as they get to know the four dimensions, they start to apply DiSC more informally and intuitively. Over time, DiSC becomes part of the way they work. Managers have commented:

- "Because of DiSC, I have my antenna up more often. I tune in to how other people are reacting to what I'm saying."
- "To me, DiSC means: Ask, don't tell."
- "DiSC defuses a lot of situations that could have been tense because I understand why other people are reacting as they are. They aren't trying to be jerks. It isn't personal."
- "DiSC has helped me develop emotional intelligence."
- "It's about awareness."

DiSC is indeed about awareness. Simple yet powerful, DiSC has helped millions of people develop awareness of themselves and others. You, too, can use this tool to become a 4-dimensional manager who can effectively manage anyone, anywhere, anytime.

The Combination DiSC Patterns

DI
ACTIVE AND LEADING

If your adjusted score for D is the same or higher than your adjusted score for I in this situation, read this DI pattern. If your I is higher, read the ID pattern

In this situation, you are probably feeling confident and are relying on yourself to get things done. You feel you have status and influence. You have a chance to be visible to others and to move quickly toward your goals. You're high-energy. Competition gives you a rush that helps you work well under pressure and in difficult situations.

Getting a lot done. If your goals are the group's goals, you'll be very productive. If there isn't a declared leader for the task, you'll probably persuade the group they need one, and you're it. In a crisis, you're the one who can make quick decisions.

Others having trouble keeping up? With all of your restless energy, you're not about to quit once you start something. People who are following your lead may not be able to keep up. You may

DI Style

Motivates You
- Leading the group
- Setting your own course
- Moving quickly
- Making decisions

Demotivates You
- Detailed directions or instructions
- Putting up with things you don't like
- No opportunities to lead or speak up
- Not being where the action is

Your Preferred Environment
- Working with people who share your interests and goals
- Status and visibility
- Open communications

You Avoid or Dislike
- Strict rules and regulations
- Lack of creativity
- Resistance to new approaches
- Detailed, slow-paced projects
- Isolation
- Negativity

To Be More Effective
- Try to be more open to the ideas of others.
- Resist the "I'll just do it myself" syndrome and channel your energy into inspiring others to achieve common goals.

then decide to just do it yourself; you think you're helping them out, but they may think you've lost interest in them or their contributions.

If you turn up your Influence dimension, you can keep the others on board. You need them. If you don't have followers, you can't lead. Channeling your energy into inspiring others will pay off big time.

Where the action is. You feel miserable when you don't see any opportunity to lead or speak up. You need freedom to be creative and try new approaches. Detailed, slow-paced projects drive you up a wall. It's tough not to walk away.

Valuing your independence. You prefer to do things your own way. After you and others agree on a goal, you want the freedom to reach it as you think best.

ID
EXPRESSIVE AND INVOLVED

If your adjusted score for I is the same or higher than your adjusted score for D in this situation, read this ID pattern. If your D is higher, read the DI pattern.

In this situation, you value relationships more than achievements. You probably express your ideas freely and find that others respond warmly. You know you can help resolve conflicts and make things better for everyone. If you enjoy the project, you'll give it everything you've got.

Throwing yourself into the situation. Whenever you're involved in something new, you get fired up. You volunteer ideas and encourage others to do the same. You could talk about the project day and night. Your enthusiasm draws others to support the project. But if others don't follow your lead, you can become discouraged and distracted. A lukewarm audience is devastating. You *expect* others will like what you like.

ID Style

Motivates You
- Building good working relationships
- Generating support for new challenges
- Contributing to the success of the group
- Direct responsibility for outcomes

Demotivates You
- Routine tasks and procedures
- Little interaction with others
- Others lack enthusiasm or interest

Your Preferred Environment
- New and exciting projects
- Conflicts are dealt with openly
- Recognition for your efforts

You Avoid or Dislike
- Inflexible rules
- Detailed or in-depth analysis
- Questioning of your ideas or judgment

To Be More Effective
- In times of change, you can help others see the benefits and encourage their involvement.
- While people enjoy your support and energy, they may want you to do your part in attending to more detailed or mundane aspects of a task.
- Don't let enthusiasm be mistaken for glory-grabbing; let others know that you think success depends on everyone.

You work the big picture. If someone wants a detailed, in-depth analysis, you'll rebel. Variety and fun keep your energy high. If a situation calls for frequent change, you'll stay interested and involved. Consider asking someone else to check things over now and then, because you might overlook details in your eagerness to move forward.

DS
SELF-MOTIVATED AND HELPFUL

In this situation, you're doing a balancing act between your determined, decisive, impatient tendencies and your desire to be helpful. You don't need to be popular, but you do like to work well with people. You want to do things that benefit others.

You may have worked your way up to a top level in a volunteer or fraternal organization because you're self-motivated and willing to help people. When your church, synagogue, or PTA needs someone to head a fund-raiser or plan the fall bazaar, they think of you first. You know just what to do, dig right in, recruit others, and then probably do a good share of the work—not for the glory of it, but because you believe in it, and it needs to be done.

Missing your other side. You are self-motivated, aggressive, and willing to take risks. You are also friendly, conscientious, and considerate of others. Because you're helpful and quiet, people often fail to recognize your strength and bravery. On the other hand, anyone who sees you acting decisively may not notice that you are a friendly, considerate person, too. People who make snap judgments generally slot you as one or the other, but you're actually both.

You take the initiative, but don't make waves. You see yourself as easy to get along with and respectful of others. While you don't want to cause problems, you will take action when action is needed—but you'll do it your way.

DS Style

Motivates You
- Personal commitment to the goal
- A balance of independent work and collaboration
- Keeping things moving
- Personal accountability

Demotivates You
- When people's feelings don't count
- When quality is ignored
- Open conflict
- Aggressive competition

Your Preferred Environment
- There's a clear direction
- Doing things well counts
- Respect for diverse needs

You Avoid or Dislike
- Asking for help, even when it is needed
- Answering a lot of questions about your approach
- Embarrassing situations
- Conflict

To Be More Effective
- Because you take the initiative, some people may miss your supportive side; keep a balance.
- Give others the chance to help you.
- You tend to be self-critical; listening to feedback of others can help you gain perspective and ease your stress.

A person who tended to use this response pattern was hired to head a bookkeeping department. She saw right away that everyone needed further computer training, but the company couldn't spare anyone from the job just now. So she made up tip sheets every week and quietly placed them on each keyboard. Even though she didn't put her name on them, people guessed who did it and appreciated her help.

Potential for burnout. You have high personal performance standards and you feel strongly that you'll let others down if you don't do your best. You often feel guilty when things don't run perfectly.

You may have workaholic tendencies. If you don't keep up with your friends or neglect your family, there goes your support system. *Support?* It may not have occurred to you that you need anyone's help. While this can be a strength when you need to work intensively by yourself, everyone needs help from time to time. You've helped others out so many times that they'll probably be glad to return the favor—but you have to ask.

DC
SELF-RELIANT AND ANALYTICAL

You feel that this situation requires you to be analytical and to trust your own judgment. Task-oriented, you may seem aloof; indeed, you seldom ask others for advice. You have strong points of view and will defend them if challenged. You're probably working hard on what you strongly believe is the right course of action because you've taken the time to think it through.

Seeing what others overlook. The quality of your work often meets or exceeds the project's requirements. In addition, you may be putting a lot of thought into solving problems. You have a gift for predicting trouble before it happens because you see issues others have missed.

DC Style

Motivates You

- Situations in which quality and accuracy are important
- Having time to think things through
- Working independently
- Doing your part

Demotivates You

- Sharing control over tasks you feel best qualified to handle
- Waiting for others to do their part

Your Preferred Environment

- Commitment to quality
- Time to examine issues from multiple perspectives
- Clear rules, procedures, and objectives
- High performance standards

You Avoid or Dislike

- Impulsive actions and quick decisions
- Group analysis
- Getting the advice of others

To Be More Effective

- Ask questions and offer advice throughout the process, not just at critical or stressful points.
- Though you know your plan is right, check in with others and bring them on board.

Sticking to your guns. You have strong ideas about right and wrong; there are rarely shades of gray on your palette. You've thought things through, and you're sure your course of action is right, but others may think you're being stubborn. To help them see things from your point of view, explain how you got from point A to point B.

You know your worth. If you have advanced training or years of experience, you probably feel that you know more than others do. While you're willing to offer advice, your skills may be best applied to tasks you can do on your own. Working alone allows you to put your analytical skills to good use. You probably have earned a reputation for producing excellent results. It's worth giving you the freedom to think things through and consider a task from several angles.

If a project depends on input from others as well as yourself, you're likely to be frustrated by having to share control and waiting for others to do their part. You will keep your mouth closed, but if you feel they're hurting the quality of the project, you'll quietly walk out.

SI
SUPPORTIVE AND FLEXIBLE

If your adjusted score for S is the same or higher than your adjusted score for I in this situation, read this profile. If your I is higher, read the IS pattern.

In this situation, you value relationships and are focused on supporting other people. You don't need to be the center of attention. You're devoted to serving others. Your primary goal is to promote harmony and get along with others.

You want everyone to be friends. You're probably doing all you can to keep this situation pleasant. When other people get angry

SI Style

Motivates You
- Positive teamwork
- Serving others
- Building good relationships
- Others depending on you

Demotivates You
- Isolated projects
- Competition
- Tension or hostility

Your Preferred Environment
- Value placed on collaboration and harmony
- Tactful, respectful communication

You Avoid or Dislike
- Being the center of attention
- Confrontations and tense situations
- Saying no, even if it's in your best interest

To Be More Effective
- Your flexibility can be valuable in times of change if you do not go overboard to accommodate a decision you think is not in the group's best interests.
- You are generous in your support of others, but you need to speak up if you feel others are taking advantage of you.
- Because you appear calm, others may think you can handle anything; be aware of your sources of stress and take care of yourself.

or impatient, your comfortable manner may calm them. You want to get along with others. You stand back and let others lead you toward a solution. Your calm manner may lead people to think you can handle any conflict, but the truth is that you want to avoid confrontations and keep things pleasant. You aren't afraid to speak up when it feels safe; when conflict or rejection is likely, you stay silent.

A generous spirit. You are willing to have others depend on you, and you feel rewarded simply by knowing you have helped. The lives of many people will be enriched in large or small ways by your generosity.

IS
ENCOURAGING AND COOPERATIVE

If your adjusted score for I is the same or higher than your adjusted score for S in this situation, read this profile. If your S is higher, read the SI pattern.

In this situation, you want to build relationships, especially ones that can serve your purpose. You recognize the value of social exchange and think that helping others may help you. You are a true networker. If you're playing a leadership role, you value other people's input and encourage them to grow. Others may seek your coaching because you're so easygoing and friendly. You can play an important role in bringing your own and others' concerns into the open.

Please don't cling! People feel comfortable asking for your advice. This is fine with you up to a point, but you don't want to listen to other people talk about their problems all the time. Your "How are you today?" is not meant to invite confidences about cranky co-workers or personal problems, let alone a recitation of health problems. You feel uneasy when others start depending on you. You aren't eager to take on the role of a personal counselor or mentor.

IS Style

Motivates You
- Working on a team
- Leading or influencing a group
- Growing and learning
- Developing new relationships that will be helpful to your purposes or your career

Demotivates You
- Lack of visibility or recognition
- Being burdened with other people's feelings or problems

Your Preferred Environment
- Secure and open
- Pleasant and trusting
- Rewards and appreciation are expressed

You Avoid or Dislike
- Listening to or being expected to solve other people's problems
- Having others depend on you too much
- Arguing

To Be More Effective
- While you don't like conflict, you can play an important role in bringing your own and others' concerns out into the open.
- Your people skills and desire to accomplish goals can make you a valuable coach in certain circumstances.

Arguments bother you. You aren't afraid to speak up about an issue when you feel it's safe to do so. However, you are reluctant to make your wants known when you're not sure how they'll be received. Also, it's hard for you to make a decision if the outcome is likely to be unpopular.

TACTFUL AND OBSERVANT

How you behave in this situation depends on whether you're focusing on people or tasks. When relating to co-workers and friends, you tend to be flexible, tactful, and reliable. When focusing on a task, *you really focus on the task,* paying attention to the details. Either way, you are conscientious. Your insights, enthusiasm, and loyalty are valuable contributions to a group. Since you're usually confident and outgoing, you are good with customers or the public.

A valuable team player. While you want to do detailed, accurate work, at the same time you are flexible, nondefensive, and willing to try new methods. While maintaining your own high standards, you also think about the needs of others. Put it together, and it adds up to a well-balanced and effective team player. You *like* teamwork, too, though you also want time alone to concentrate on details.

Easygoing and reliable. You produce consistent, quality work without asking for praise or reward. Still, it feels rewarding when you do good work that others value.

Waiting it out. You don't like to start a conflict, so you may put up with disappointments and troubles in the hope that the situation will get better. In the meantime, others may take advantage of you. Instead of waiting for something to change, consider expressing your ideas and insights. Your enthusiasm and people skills will help you. It is sometimes necessary to be proactive.

IC Style

Motivates You
- A mixture of working independently and working with others
- Situations in which accuracy and quality matter

Demotivates You
- Lack of acknowledgment of your consistently good work
- No opportunity to work on independent projects
- Being taken advantage of
- Tolerance of sloppy work

Your Preferred Environment
- Loyalty to people and the organization
- High standards and integrity valued
- Contributions noticed and appreciated
- Effective and flexible teams

You Avoid or Dislike
- Acting without prior analysis
- Unexpected changes
- Arguments

To Be More Effective
- Instead of standing by until something changes, use your warmth and enthusiasm to help you express your own ideas and insights for your own good and the good of the group.
- Your adaptability is a great strength in times of change, but don't let it stop you from taking the initiative when you need to.

SC
RESPECTFUL AND ACCURATE

In this situation, you are careful with both people and tasks. You behave respectfully and don't cause any problems or draw attention to yourself.

You may be an important source of solutions. Because you tend to be quiet and unassuming, even shy, others may not give you enough credit for what you know. You pay close attention to issues and analyze them in detail. You want to understand the issues. You may be able to draw on your knowledge to solve problems. Although you like to avoid conflicts, your insights may help resolve them in subtle ways that don't threaten others.

Don't tell me you need it tomorrow. Short deadlines and rushed decisions are stressful for you. When possible, let others know up front how much time you need to get your work done well and on schedule. Your need for clarity and certainty can frustrate others when a decision or action is needed *now*. Complete accuracy is not always necessary; a degree of risk may be acceptable when time is short and decisions must be made. You can help minimize that risk, and increase your comfort, by drawing on lessons learned while analyzing similar situations in the past.

DIS
COMFORTABLE AND ENGAGED

You are probably feeling confident and happy in this situation. You make the job fun. You encourage others to jump in. You see even difficult situations in a positive way. You're motivated by a desire to help and a willingness to do whatever it takes to accomplish things for yourself and for others.

SC Style

Motivates You
- Ample time to analyze the issues
- Consideration for people's time and concerns
- Clear, meaningful, specific instructions

Demotivates You
- Rush assignments
- Lack of concern for the impact of tasks on people
- Unclear direction

Your Preferred Environment
- Stable
- Clear goals and objectives
- Clearly defined expectations and standards

You Avoid or Dislike
- Being at the center of things
- Having to verbalize thoughts and feelings
- Crash projects
- Quick decisions
- Surprises.

To Be More Effective
- Even if there hasn't been time to do analysis in advance, be willing to contribute your insights and solutions.
- If you think you can help, offer your ideas—even if you haven't been asked.
- Accept that some risk is okay when time is short and a decision has to be made.

DIS Style

Motivates You

- A positive outlook
- Fun
- Encouraging a group
- When contributions are recognized

Demotivates You

- Detailed tasks
- Lack of concern or appreciation for people
- Little opportunity to work with others

Your Preferred Environment

- Working with others toward common goals
- Good visibility
- Enjoying yourself
- Positive attitudes
- Success is celebrated and rewarded

You Avoid or Dislike

- Detailed, tedious projects
- Isolation
- Negativity

To Be More Effective

- Accept the fact that while a positive outlook is good, work is not always going to be fun.
- Resist wearing yourself out by spending too much energy encouraging others.
- Remember to reward yourself.

Power hungry? You're probably popular with most people. However, some people may be jealous of the attention you're receiving. They may think you are power hungry and silently resent you.

Spreading yourself too thin. You may feel that your most important contribution in this situation is to make others feel welcome and to help them see that they can achieve their goals. That is admirable, but being attentive and responsive to too many people may eventually wear you out.

Sweating the details. You dislike details, so you avoid them. Others may feel they're left attending to things you should be doing. Consider using your powers of persuasion to get the help you need with all those important details.

Treat time. Find ways to reward yourself, as well as others, when work is tedious or morale is low. When a goal is met, there's no doubt who will be leading the celebration!

IDC
CONFIDENT AND DETERMINED

In this situation, you want to be in charge. You have a strong sense of what has to be done and are committed to your own approach. You want time alone to figure out a plan; then you want full authority to carry it out. You're confident in your ability to meet the challenges of the situation, and you don't let anyone or anything get in your way. You are often the first person to spot a need for change, and you can lead the way through the transition.

I'll take care of it. You're confident, outspoken, and energetic. You've identified the changes needed, and you're determined to make them. This confidence and determination can be a positive driving force, but it may also be mistaken for arrogance.

IDC Style

Motivates You
- Being in charge
- Taking on new challenges
- Developing solutions

Demotivates You
- Not having authority
- Not dealing openly with issues
- Co-workers who aren't concerned about quality or doing things right

Your Preferred Environment
- Demanding projects
- Helping others achieve clearly articulated goals

You Avoid or Dislike
- Not thinking things through
- People who are not willing to push forward
- Questioning of your ideas or judgment

To Be More Effective
- Not everyone can move toward change and goals as quickly as you—take the time to bring them on board. You can't lead if no one is following.
- Communicate your ideas and analysis to the group, to get everyone to buy in to your plan.
- Demonstrate that you're willing to listen to and consider the ideas and opinions of others.

Anything worth doing is worth doing right. You look at the big picture, but you also manage the details. You keep sight of your goals and are unlikely to overlook any detail important to achieving them. Your determination will result in meeting those goals.

Left in the dust. It's possible that others are feeling left behind. If you ignore other people's ideas and opinions, they will feel discounted and will lose interest.

DSC
RESPONSIBLE AND ACCURATE

You've been inspired by a challenging situation. Not content with the way things are, you're taking responsibility for changing them. You're willing to devote your efforts and skills to making things turn out well for everyone.

You value doing things well and are not likely to overlook important details. If the situation is uncertain or risky, the group needs someone like you who's willing to look for the answers methodically and objectively. With your ability to learn from experience, you can see what needs to be done to meet the group's objectives.

Beast of burden. You're probably assuming heavy responsibility in this situation. You may feel, resentfully, that others aren't pulling their weight. Ask yourself whether you are letting others know where you need help. Also, practice saying no. Let others carry some of the load.

On task—perhaps a bit too much? You tend to put the task before people's feelings. Things must be done well, even if others feel pushed around. At times, you get so focused on the work at hand that others may think you aren't concerned about their roles. And they may be right.

DSC Style

Motivates You

- Improving things and achieving goals
- Using your skills and experience
- Being personally accountable

Demotivates You

- Unclear goals
- Lack of attention to detail
- Ignoring quality

Your Preferred Environment

- Clear rules and processes
- Clearly communicated expectations
- Emphasis on doing things well

You Avoid or Dislike

- Poorly defined expectations and responsibilities for yourself and others
- Being left out of key decisions
- People who don't carry their share of the workload
- Conflict

To Be More Effective

- Share your expertise so others can learn from your ability to do things well.
- Let others know what you need, so you won't have to carry too much of the burden.
- If you tend to be self-critical, listen to the feedback of others to gain perspective and ease your stress.

Your toughest critic. Because you have high standards for performance, as well as a deep sense of responsibility, you tend to be overly critical of yourself.

ISC
RESPONSIVE AND THOUGHTFUL

In this situation, you're getting things done accurately and effectively, while remaining supportive of others.

Inspiring others to keep going. You enjoy being a team member and helping the other members succeed. However, you don't want to be the leader; you don't want to be held accountable for major decisions or taking risks. Though you don't want to take the lead, your accommodating approach can inspire others to keep going in hard times.

Don't rush me. When it's your choice, you prefer to have time to think things through. This means you may bring valuable insights to the process. However, you may find that your reluctance to move fast frustrates others. When others don't want to wait, they'll make a decision without your input.

Not always rosy. Your friendly attitude may lead others to believe that everything's just fine, even when you're not satisfied. You're probably reluctant to speak up on your own behalf, so others may take advantage of you without realizing it.

ISC Style

Motivates You
- Interacting with and supporting others
- A chance to contribute to projects that require attention to detail
- Being appreciated for your willingness to make the best of things

Demotivates You
- Responsibility for leading others
- Working alone
- Having to speak up on behalf of your personal needs or interests

Your Preferred Environment
- Comfortable and cooperative
- Pleasant and trusting
- Opportunities to encourage others

You Avoid or Dislike
- Responsibility for major decisions
- Risks
- Not having the time to think things over on your own

To Be More Effective
- You have valuable insights—speak up and share them.
- Apply your ability to inspire to keep others going when things get tough.

Additional DiSC Tool

good listener		want to make the rules	
put up with things I don't like		go straight ahead with projects	
willing to follow orders		act in a forceful way	
will go along with others		want to win	
think of others before I decide		will be the first to act	
willing to help		do not give in	
understand others' feelings		people see me as powerful	
nice to other people		sure of myself	
have warm feelings for people		want to be in charge	
let others lead		like to take action	
don't like to cause problems		quick to act	
don't make demands of people		feel strong	
Total column 1		**Total column 2**	
Subtract	-1	Add	+2
Score	●	Score	▬

Working across the four columns on both pages, write after each phrase the number that best describes you in this situation. 1 = Very inaccurate or does not apply 2 = Inaccurate
3 = Neither accurate nor inaccurate 4 = Accurate 5 = Very accurate

like to do things accurately		wide variety of friends	
like doing things the right way		liked by others	
do things right the first time		like to meet people	
think of what makes sense		fun to be with	
like to be precise		see things positively	
shy with others		feel contented	
good at analyzing things		happy and carefree	
think things through		liven things up	
keep things to myself		feel relaxed most of the time	
think things over carefully		happy most of the time	
don't like too much attention		find it easy to meet strangers	
don't say much in a group		communicate in a lively manner	
Total column 3		**Total column 4**	
	+0	Subtract	-2
Score	(	Score	◆

The Research behind DiSC

By taking the DiSC profile in *The 4-Dimensional Manager,* you have joined the more than forty million people worldwide who have used Inscape Publishing's DiSC products. Our DiSC products are based on the work of William Moulton Marston, Ph.D., as published in his 1928 book *The Emotions of Normal People.* Marston set out to learn if there were systematic ways in which people responded to their environment. He was interested not only in how people behaved, but in how their behavior changed from situation to situation. Through his research, he hoped to increase people's understanding of themselves and others while decreasing misunderstandings. He found that two kinds of perception are particularly useful for explaining people's response in a particular situation: perception of environment and perception of one's self. As Marston observed, these two kinds of perception interact to describe an individual's response to a situation.

Dominance: When the environment is perceived as *unfavorable* and the person feels *more powerful* than the environment, he or she responds with Dominance. The person will likely try to change, fix, or control the situation.

Influence: When the environment is perceived as *favorable* and the person feels *more powerful* than the environment, he or she experiences a desire to Influence. The person will likely try to bring others around to his or her point of view.

Supportiveness: When the environment is perceived as *favorable* and the person feels *less powerful* than the environment, he or she experiences an opportunity to be Supportive. The person will likely try to keep the situation as it is and support those in need.

Conscientiousness: When the environment is perceived as *unfavorable* and the person feels *less powerful* than the environment, he or she responds with Conscientiousness. The person will likely set clear rules within the situation and work very hard to follow them.

Ongoing Research

While Marston created the DISC model, he never developed an instrument by which to measure it. For more than thirty years, Inscape Publishing has researched and refined the original DISC theory to maximize its impact and accuracy. Like our other DiSC products, the DiSC instrument in this book is based on Inscape Publishing's most current research.

The first thing to consider when examining the research behind an instrument is the type of people who participated in the research—in other words, the sample. The sample determines for whom the instrument is appropriate. For example, if the sample included only white male accountants from Kansas, then the instrument would be appropriate for use only by white male accountants from Kansas. Inscape Publishing made sure that our research sample was representative of people of different ages and racial backgrounds and from a wide variety of occupations and geographical locations. In other words, we made sure that our research sample represented you so that you would find the instrument and feedback in *The 4-Dimensional Manager* helpful.

The next item to be considered in research is the instrument's reliability and its validity. Reliability indicates whether a scale is measuring a construct (i.e., a concept such as dominance) *consistently.* Reliabilities are determined using a statistic called Cronbach's alpha coefficient. Scale reliabilities must be equal to or greater than .70 in order for a scale to be acceptable for use. Scale reliability coefficients for the DiSC instrument in this book range from .77 to .85.

Validity is whether a scale measures *what it is said to measure.* Validity was emphasized in creating both the scales and the response pattern feedback. The validity of the scales is supported by two types of statistical analyses: factor analysis and multidimensional scaling. The feedback provided in this book is also based on research and thus follows the actual responses of persons who obtain a similar profile, rather than being the "best guess" of the publisher.

Inscape Publishing's products are known for the sound research used to create and validate them. Our DiSC products are also distinctive in that they capture the situational nature of people's responses. Not all situations are alike. As situations vary, so do our responses. The extensive research used to create Inscape Publishing's DiSC products allows the products to capture the differences in our responses from one situation to another. This, in turn, allows the respondents to capitalize on the full range of responses available to them as they pursue their goals and seek a better understanding of themselves.

Appropriate Use

The instrument is appropriate for individuals who are eighteen years of age and older and interested in learning more about themselves. A seventh-grade reading level is necessary to fully understand both the response items and pattern interpretation.

The main purpose of the instrument is to assist individuals on their own path of human growth and discovery. We believe that "you are the expert on you." We assume people are capable of setting their own goals, directing their efforts, and appraising results. We advise people to read their feedback and consider it carefully. After doing so, people are encouraged to make use of the information they find helpful and to disregard the information that is not.

Neither this book nor the instrument it contains is meant to be a substitute for mental health services. It is assumed that those completing the DiSC profile are in reasonably sound mental health; none of the interpretations that are available offer guidance in dealing with significant emotional issues. Persons seeking mental health counseling should obtain that help from a licensed counselor or therapist.

About Inscape and the Inscape Guides

Inscape is the world's leading independent developer and publisher of research-based personal learning tools for business and personal life, including the DiSC-based *Personal Profile System*. Our tools have helped more than fifty million people discover and make the most of their strengths and work together more successfully. Because of our commitment to the highest standards of validity, reliability, and ongoing research across diverse populations, for nearly thirty years Inscape Publishing has been the first choice among training and development professionals for learning self-assessments.

For the first time, Inscape is developing our most popular learning tools into a series of business books. *The 4-Dimensional Manager* follows the first book in the series, *I'm Stuck, You're Stuck: Break Through to Better Work Relationships and Results by Discovering Your DiSC Behavioral Style.* A DiSC-based book on selling is in the works, as well as books based on our tools for building teams, developing leadership, and managing expectations. The Inscape Guides will offer people a chance to learn about themselves, value differences in others, and then map their own ways to improved communication, fewer conflicts, top performance, career growth, and personal satisfaction.

Please visit www.inscapepublishing.com to find out how you can learn more about yourself through our online DiSC experience.

If you are interested in learning more about Inscape and its products, or would like to connect with an authorized Inscape facilitator or trainer, please contact us at: Inscape Publishing, 6465 Wayzata Blvd., Suite #800, Minneapolis, MN 55426–1725. Attention: Consumer Publishing.

About the Author

Julie Straw is Vice President of Training and Communications for Inscape Publishing. She is a frequent speaker at national training and development conferences on the topic of using DiSC to manage and motivate a changing workforce. Previously, she held management positions in training, product development, and business development. She holds an M.B.A. from the University of St. Thomas in Minneapolis, Minnesota.

She lives in Maple Grove, Minnesota, with her husband, Jim, and her son, Andy. This is her first book.

About the Writer

Alison Brown Cerier is a book developer. Her company, Alison Brown Cerier Book Development, Inc., is managing, editing, and designing the Inscape Guides. For a dozen years, the company has produced nonfiction books for major publishers and with such organizations as the American Medical Association, Reader's Digest, and the New York Public Library. Previously, she was an editor for the publishers William Morrow and Doubleday. She lives in Plymouth, Minnesota.

Berrett-Koehler Publishers

Berrett-Koehler is an independent publisher of books, audios, and other publications at the leading edge of new thinking and innovative practice on work, business, management, leadership, stewardship, career development, human resources, entrepreneurship, and global sustainability.

Since the company's founding in 1992, we have been committed to creating a world that works for all by publishing books, periodicals, and other publications that help us to integrate our values with our work and work lives, and to create more humane and effective organizations.

We have chosen to focus on the areas of work, business, and organizations, because these are central elements in many people's lives today. Furthermore, the work world is going through tumultuous changes, from the decline of job security to the rise of new structures for organizing people and work. We believe that change is needed at all levels—individual, organizational, community, and global—and our publications address each of these levels.

Previously Published Inscape Guide

I'm Stuck, You're Stuck
*Break Through to Better Work Relationships and Results by
   Discovering Your DiSC Behavioral Style*
By Tom Ritchey with Alan Axelrod
ISBN 1-57675-133-3 $15.95